WinZip
for Beginners

Brian Howard

Abacus

Contents

Introduction

When Jim Oldfield told me he was working on a book titled *WinZip for Beginners*, my first thought was "Did I do something wrong?"

WinZip is supposed to be easy for beginners to use; you aren't supposed to need a lot of documentation to get started. But as I thought about it, in light of the fact that there are bookshelves full of titles on Office 97, and that Microsoft probably spends more on Office 97 usability in one year than WinZip will ever earn, I started feeling good about the book. After all, if someone writes a book about your product, it says something for the popularity of the software.

With more than 3 million downloads from just one web site (www.download.com) in a little over a year, WinZip has come a long way from where it started, back in 1990.

WinZip grew from a project to teach myself how to program for a graphic user interface. [Editor's note: A graphic user interface (GUI) lets one navigate a computer via pictures and icons, like Windows, e.g.] At the time, I was just starting to use the OS/2 Presentation Manager. I often found myself getting frustrated with the File Manager, because I had to switch from the graphical shell to the DOS command prompt in order to unzip files. I decided to solve this problem by writing a graphical "shell" to zip and unzip files without jumping back to the DOS command prompt. Everyone that saw the result liked it, and I released PMZIP as shareware in late 1990. I got favorable responses from people that used it, but back in 1990 OS/2 was not very successful, and PMZIP was not a big commercial success.

By January of 1991 I realized that much of the world was moving to Microsoft's Windows, and I'd better learn how it worked. My first Windows programming project was to port PMZIP to Windows, and in early 1991 I released WinZip 1.0. It had the same features as PMZIP but was much a lot more successful, no doubt because of the larger potential user base.

When I first released WinZip I had no idea how much time it would take. I learned that while writing a basic ZIP shell is not a huge project, turning it into something thousands of people use is a lot harder, and requires continuous revisions and improvements. I've released major updates every year and minor updates more frequently, adding features, integrating with new operating environments, etc. A few of the more important revisions include supporting additional file formats (the original version 1.0 only worked with .ZIP files), built-in compression (early versions relied upon external compression programs), integration with new operating systems (first Windows 3.1, then Windows NT, and latest Windows 95—including support for long filenames and other 32-bit features), and perhaps most popular: the WinZip Wizard, which greatly simplifies unzipping files for novices. Though I obviously can't commit to any future WinZip features in this fast-changing computer environment, expect future versions to be even easier use, have more file compatibility and maybe hold a few surprises.

Shareware

Shareware is a distribution method that gives users a chance to try a fully functional copy of a software package before buying it. Rather than spending a lot of money on expensive advertising and retail packaging, shareware products can be launched with a few uploads, which was ideal for the first versions of WinZip.

With the growth of the internet, this "try before you buy" method of marketing has become more and more popular, but back in 1990, very few serious developers would release fully functional versions of their software for a free trial. Now even Microsoft has versions of Office available for trial runs.

Acknowledgments

Many people have helped make WinZip what it is, by making suggestions, helping test, reporting bugs, etc., but particular thanks go to the following individuals: Ted Abell, Robert Allen, Tom Bloch, Steve Carless, John Conde, Ora Lee Dinkins, Kent Downs, Ray Ebersole, Brian Hill, Stefan Hoffmeister, David Hofmann, Gregg Hommel, Oyvind Kaldestad, Kevin Kearney, Marion Kerr, Jim Larkin, John Navas, Heath Perryman, Sara Rogers, Sven Schreiber,

Chris Sells, Paul Seltzer, Barry Steinholtz, Michael Sundermann, Nick Sweeting, Peter Tanis, Roy Tate, Hans Top, Michael Weber, and Larry Wilber.

WinZip incorporates compression code by the Info-ZIP group, which is used with their permission. Special thanks to the entire Info-Zip group, in particular to Jean-loup Gailly, Greg Roelofs, and Mark Adler. The original Info-Zip sources are freely available from CompuServe in the pcprog forum and by anonymous ftp from the Internet site ftp.uu.net:/pub/archiving/zip.

Thanks to Jean-loup Gailly for permission to use portions of his GZIP source in WinZip. The original sources to GZIP are available on the Internet as prep.ai.mit.edu:/pub/gnu/gzip-*.tar.

Decoding subroutines based on the UUDeview package (c) Frank Pilhofer.

Special thanks to Steve Queen for his feedback on the WinZip user interface, and to Edward Stumpf for his many suggestions and his help testing WinZip.

Note On Registering Your Copy Of Winzip

To register your copy of WinZip that is on the companion CD-ROM, please contact Niko Mak Computing at www.winzip.com or use the following information.

Place credit card orders by phone, fax, e-mail, or postal mail through PsL, a credit card ordering service. The best way to reach PsL is by fax to 1-713-524-6398 or by Internet mail to 71355.470@compuserve.com. You can also call PsL at 1-800-242-4PsL(4775) or 1-713-524-6394 between 8:30 am and 5:00 pm CST Monday-Friday, except holidays.

Send credit card orders via postal mail to PsL at P.O. at Box 35705, Houston, TX 77235 USA. Please be sure to include a completed credit card order form with your order (available at www.winzip.com).

Nico Mak Computing, Inc., cannot be reached at the numbers above. These numbers are for PsL, a third-party service which only takes credit card orders.

Any questions about the status of the shipment of an order, refunds, registration options, product details, technical support, volume discounts, dealer pricing, site licenses, etc., must be directed to Nico Mak Computing. You can send Internet mail to help@winzip.com; their goal is to respond to all e-mail inquiries within one business day. You can also send postal mail to Nico Mak Computing, P.O. Box 540, Mansfield, CT 06268, USA.

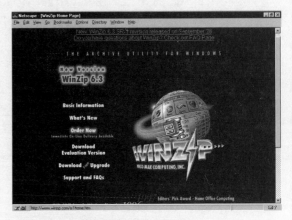

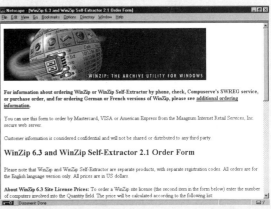

www.winzip.com

Chapter 1

What Is A Zipped File?

WinZip for Beginners

B asically, a zipped file is a copy of another file. The difference between this copy and the original is that the data in the file has been compressed (or shrunk) in the zipped file.

If you have browsed the Internet or traded computer files with friends or colleagues, you have probably encountered "zipped" files. Zipping files is a convenient way to organize and transport computer information. Almost any computer file can be compressed (or zipped). Depending on the type of file being compressed, zipping can shrink a file's size by a few bytes or more than fifty percent! If you have received one of these zipped files (identified by the .ZIP file extension), you'll need a zipping utility like WinZip to unzip (or *decompress*, or *unpack*) it before you can use its contents.

Why are files zipped? For three very good reasons:

1. Save space

2. Save time

3. Clear organization

What Is A Zipped File?

ZIP files are substantially smaller than their uncompressed counterparts. This means you can save many more files in the same space on your backup media and your local hard drive(s). Zipping is a great way to store programs and files that are only rarely used.

Because zipped files are smaller, they take much less time (and bandwidth) when being copied across the Internet or a local network. Internet downloads occur much quicker thanks to zipping.

Zipping can also help organize your files. For example, say you've written biographies of American presidents, and you want want to share some of these with a friend. You could copy 12 individual files (TRUMAN.TXT, CARTER.TXT, REAGAN.TXT, etc.) onto several floppy disks or send each life story as a separate e-mail attachment. With WinZip, however, you can pack all of the biographies into a single ZIP file (PRESIDENTS.ZIP) and send one file to your friend through the Internet or on one floppy. When your friend receives the file, he or she easily unzips PRESIDENTS.ZIP to read each of the .TXT files. This uses one easy-to-identify ZIP file instead of a dozen uniquely titled files that could get scattered across a hard drive.

How does compression work?

Several strategies are used to compress computer data. In simple terms, programs are shrunk by removing empty space and by substituting short codes for long strings of commonly repeated data. For example, the Preamble of the US Constitution has a lot of empty space on the page. This makes the document more readable on paper, but has no effect on the meaning of the document. So let's get rid of that space.

WinZip for Beginners

The Constitution of the United States

PREAMBLE

We, the people of the United States, in order to form a more perfect Union, establish justice, insure domestic tranquility, provide for the common defense, promote the general welfare, and secure the blessings of liberty to ourselves and our posterity, do ordain and establish this Constitution for the United States of America.
..

Legislative powers; in whom vested
..
..
All legislative powers herein granted shall be vested in a Congress of the United States, which shall consist of a Senate and House of Representatives.
..
House of Representatives, how and by whom chosen Qualifications of a Representative. Representatives and direct taxes, how apportioned. Enumeration. Vacancies to be filled. Power of
choosing officers, and of impeachment.
..
..
The House of Representatives shall be composed of members chosen every second year by the people of the several States, and the elector in each State shall have the qualifications requisite for electors of the most numerous branch of the State Legislature.
..
No person shall be a Representative who shall not have attained the age of twenty-five years, and been seven years a citizen of the United States, and who shall not, when elected, be an inhabitant of that State in which he shall be chosen.
..
Representatives
..
and direct taxes
..
Altered by 16th Amendment
..
shall be apportioned among the several States which may be included within this Union, according to their respective numbers,
..

The Constitution of the United States#PREAMBLE#We, the people of the United States, in order to form a more perfect Union,#establish justice, insure domestic Tranquility, provide for the common#defense, promote the general welfare and secure The blessings of liberty to#ourselves and our posterity, do ordain and establish this Constitution for
#the United States of America.##Legislative powers; in whom vested##All legislative powers herein granted shall be vested in a Congress of the#United States, which shall consist of a Senate and House of Representatives.##House of Representatives, how and by whom chosen
#Qualifications of a Representative. Representatives and direct taxes,#how apportioned. Enumeration. Vacancies to be filled. Power of#choosing officers, and of impeachment.
#The House of Representatives shall be composed of members chosen#every second year by the people of the several States, and the elector in#each State shall have the qualifications requisite for electors of the most#numerous branch of the State Legislature.##No person shall be a Representative who shall not have attained the Age#of twenty-five years, and been seven years a citizen of the United States,#and Who shall not, when elected, be an inhabitant of that State in which he#shall be Chosen.##Representatives and##direct taxes
##Altered by 16th Amendment##shall be apportioned among the several#States which may be included within this Union, according to their#respective numbers.

You can see here that the text is the same, but the long spaces and paragraph breaks have been replaced by pound signs '#'. Already the document has shrunk by almost half. We can squeeze it further by replacing long, repeated text strings with shorter representations.

For instance, we can replace every instance of "United States" with "US," replacing 13 characters with two. "Representative" also appears often, so let's replace that with "Rp."

Throughout this excerpt, these two changes eliminate another 139 characters, further shrinking the file size. When this file is later uncompressed, the unzipping program replaces pounds '#' with paragraph marks, "US" with "United States" and "Rp" with "Representative," returning the Constitution to its previous, unzipped form.

Important Note

If you'd like to know more about compression operations and program details, check out ZIP Bible, also available from Abacus.

WinZip for Beginners

Of course, this is an oversimplification of a complex procedure, but it illustrates the basic processes that compression programs use to shrink data without losing its meaning or format.

WinZip is a very easy to use program, and you can use it effectively without inimately understanding what it does behind the scenes. As a beginners' book, we are more concerned with getting you running without bogging down in technical details.

And so, the next step to using WinZip is installing the program...

Chapter 2

Installing WinZip Shareware

WinZip for Beginners

Y ou'll discover just how easy WinZip is to use right from the beginning as you install it.

* Insert the WinZip for Beginners companion CD-ROM in the CD-ROM drive of your computer.

* Click [Start] and select the **Run...** command to open the Run dialog box.

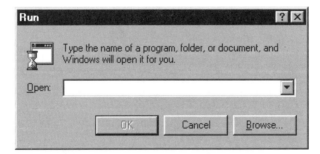

* Type D:\SETUP.EXE in the dialog box and click [OK].

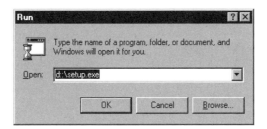

This begins the WinZip installation wizard.

* The installation program installs WinZip to C:\Program Files\WinZip by default. Click OK to accept this or type in your preferred directory path (as we did in the example below).

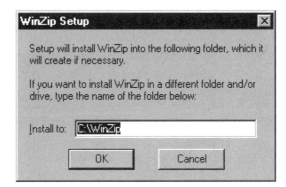

* Watch the progress of the installation in the status bar.

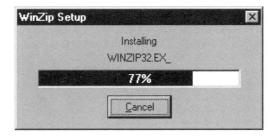

* Read about WinZip's new features on the next screen. As you read about the features, notice also that you can press F1 any time to open WinZip's Help file.

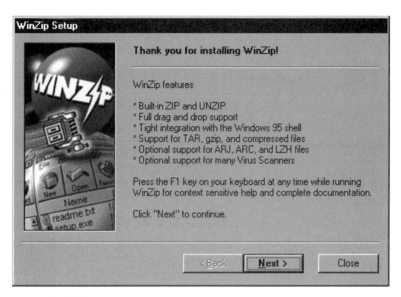

* Click [Next>] when you are ready to continue. The next screen talks about the license agreement. It's very important to read and understand this agreement.

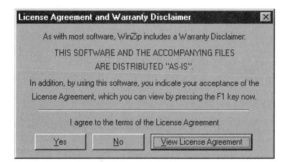

Therefore, click the [View License Agreement] button to see the entire license agreement.

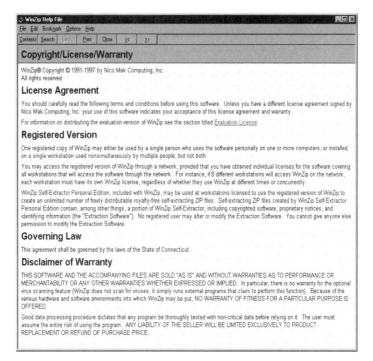

Once you've read and understand it, click the [Close] button. Then click [Yes] to agree 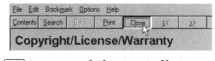 to the terms of the agreement or [No] to cancel the installation.

❋ You can start WinZip with either the Classic interface or the Wizard interface. The Wizard is better if you want to unzip files quickly or install software distributed in Zip files. (We'll explore WinZip Classic later. It's more powerful and is recommended for users familiar with Windows and Zip files. Until then, the WinZip Wizard is an easy way to learn to use WinZip's basic features.)

Click the "Start with the WinZip Wizard" option and then click [Next>].

WinZip for Beginners

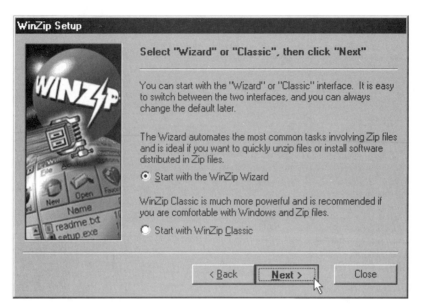

* On the next screen, select either the recommended "Search Entire Hard Disk (recommended)" or the "Quick Search (faster)" option. WinZip will then scan your computer for ZIP files, and will prompt you to add their directories to WinZip's Favorite Zip Folders list, which can be edited at any time. After choosing one of these searches, click [Next>].

The "Favorite Zip Folders" feature organizes downloads and all other Zip files into one convenient list. You can sort this list by date. This makes it easier to locate all Zip files, regardless of where they came from or where they are stored.

Installing WinZip Shareware

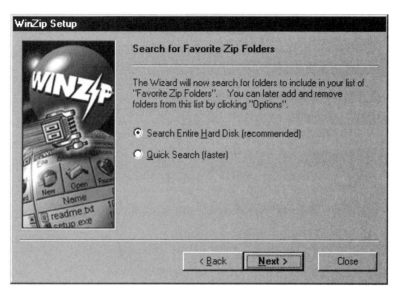

* WinZip's installation wizard finds directories labeled for downloads and others containing ZIP files. Select those you would like added to WinZip's Favorite Zip Folders list and click [OK]. If you would prefer not to add any of these to the list now, click [Cancel]. Click [Next>] to move to the next screen.

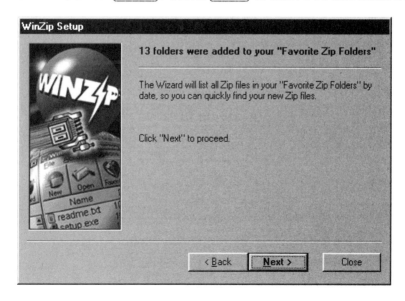

❋ Setup is now complete.

Click $\boxed{\text{Next>}}$ to launch the WinZip Wizard or $\boxed{\text{Close}}$ to exit WinZip's installation.

Uninstalling WinZip

If you should ever need to remove WinZip from your computer, this can be done easily and safely in three ways.

1. Double-click on the Uninstall WinZip icon in the WinZip program group.

Installing WinZip Shareware

2. Run WinZip with the /uninstall switch. For example, if WinZip was installed in the default directory, select [Start], Run... and type "C:\Program Files\WinZip\WinZip32.EXE /uninstall".

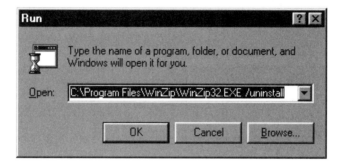

3. Use the Add/Remove Programs feature in Windows 95. Click **Start/Settings/Control Panels** and double-click the Add/Remove Programs icon. Select WinZip in the list and click [Add/Remove...].

WinZip for Beginners

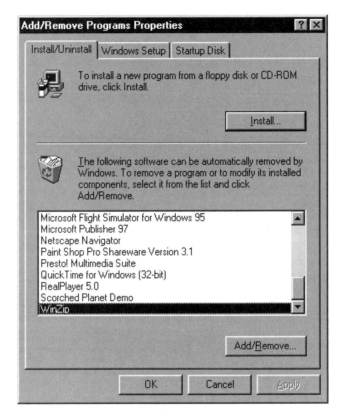

You'll see the following warning dialog box appear:

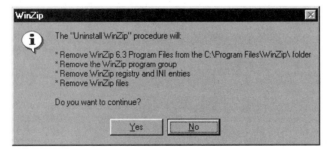

Click Yes to uninstall WinZip or No to return to Windows. If you clicked Yes to uninstall WinZip, the Uninstall WinZip procedure does the following:

* Makes certain it's safe to uninstall WinZip

* Remove WinZip File Manager Extension from WINFILE.INI (if it is installed).

* Deletes files in WinZip folder if they were installed by WinZip and if the file's date/time stamp matches WINZIP32.EXE (Windows 95 and Windows NT) or WINZIP.EXE (Windows 3.1). The WINZIP.GID, WINZIP.FTS and WINZIP.PIF files are deleted regardless of their date/time stamp.

* Removes any WinZip file associations and the [WinZip] entry from WIN.INI.

* Removes the WinZip icons and program group.

* Removes the WinZip entries from the registration database.

You will need to restart Windows for the changes to take effect.

Chapter 3

Using The WinZip Wizard

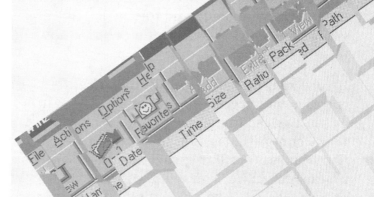

WinZip for Beginners

You are probably interested in WinZip because you need a quick and easy way to open ZIP files. Many programs, sound clips, movies and documents are available on the Web. These are almost always compressed to save space and download time. Or perhaps a friend forwarded an interesting screen saver to you in ZIP format. Before you can use any of these files you'll need to unzip them.

If your main interest in ZIP files is simply unzipping the files you receive or download, the WinZip Wizard is the easiest interface to use. Wizards are used for many computing tasks; they take users step-by-step through unfamiliar procedures. If you have just installed WinZip, you can go directly to the Wizard by clicking [Next>]. If you installed WinZip by the steps in Chapter Two, double-clicking the WinZip icon or running it from the **Start** menu will launch the WinZip Wizard. Both methods are shown to the right.

WinZip

Using The WinZip Wizard

The next screen you'll see reminds you that you're using an unregistered version of WinZip. Click the [Ordering Information] button to see how you can order the full registered version of WinZip using the Internet, phone, fax, e-mail or postal mail. See page 23 for information on ordering a registered copy of WinZip.

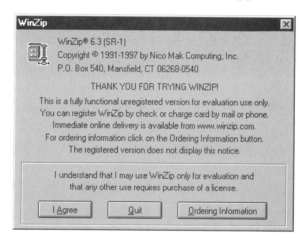

Click [I Agree] to continue or [Quit] to get out of WinZip. The next screen you'll see is the WinZip Wizard Welcome screen.

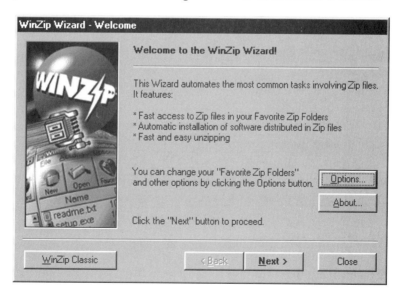

WinZip for Beginners

The starting screen introduces the WinZip Wizard and has five active buttons.

Clicking [WinZip Classic] switches WinZip to the more advanced WinZip Classic interface. We'll use the Classic interface a little later. If you want to see what it looks like, click this button now. You can return to the Wizard by clicking the Wizard button in the Classic toolbar (shown on the right).

Clicking the [Options...] button lets you review and modify the decisions you made during installation. The "Favorite Zip Folders" tab lists your WinZip favorite folders. These should be the same as your selection during installation. The "Other Zip Folders" tab lets you select a folder to be automatically added to your Favorite list when you open a zipped file from that folder.

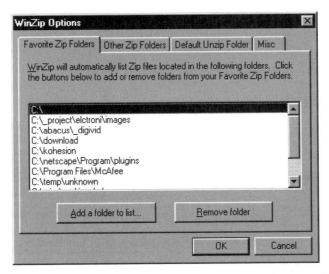

The "Favorite Zip Folders" tab lists your WinZip favorite folders.

Alternatively, select that no new folders be automatically added to your Favorite list. You can also have WinZip prompt you each time you open a ZIP file if you want that file's directory to be added to the WinZip Favorite ZIP Folders list.

Select the "Default Unzip Folder" tab to change the default folder. Select the "Misc" tab to determine whether WinZip starts with the Wizard or Classic Interface.

Click [OK] to return to the WinZip Wizard Welcome screen.

Clicking the [About...] button shows information on the version, release and contact information and five buttons for more information.

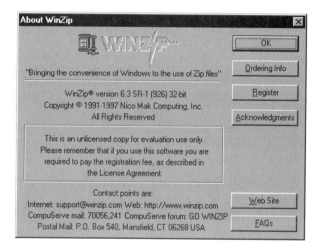

Click the [Ordering Info] button to see details on how you can order the registered version of WinZip through the mail, Web or CompuServe. Click the [License] button to open copyright, license and warranty information. Click the [Acknowledgments] button to display credits and thanks to those who helped WinZip become one of the most popular programs in the world. For the latest WinZip information, click the [Web Site] button. This will launch your Web browser and take you to the WinZip Web site (www.winzip.com).

WinZip for Beginners

You may also want to read WinZip's frequently asked questions. To do so, click the ⌊FAQs⌋ button. This opens another window where you may choose to view the FAQs on the WinZip Web site or those in the WinZip Help file.

Click ⌊OK⌋ to return to the WinZip Wizard Welcome screen. Two buttons remain on the Wizard Welcome screen. Clicking ⌊Next>⌋ takes you to the next step in the Wizard. Clicking ⌊Close⌋ exits the program.

Click ⌊Next>⌋ so WinZip can look for ZIP files in your Favorite Zip Folders.

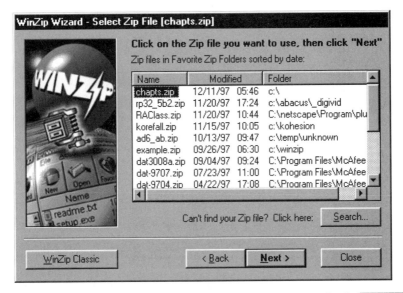

If the ZIP file you seek isn't listed in the window, click ⌊Search...⌋ and point WinZip where to find it. If you don't have a ZIP file to work with, search for "EXAMPLE.ZIP" on the WinZip for Beginners companion CD-ROM. When WinZip finds the ZIP file with which you wish to work, select it in the window and click ⌊Next>⌋.

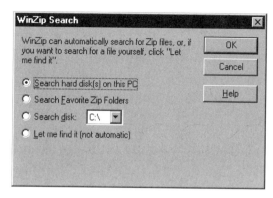

If the archive you are unzipping contains a setup or install program, the WinZip Wizard will extract all the files to a temporary folder. It will then run the install program, after which WinZip will erase the temporary files it created.

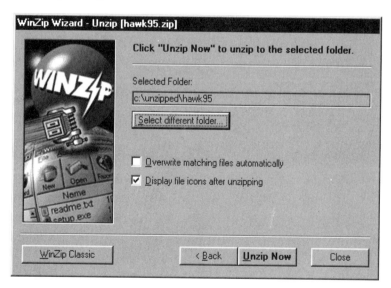

If the archive doesn't contain an installation routine, select to what folder the archive will be extracted by clicking the [Select different folder...] button.

WinZip for Beginners

You also have two more options. First, tell WinZip whether it should automatically overwrite preexisting files that have the same name as new files being unzipped. The "Overwrite matching files automatically" is a good option to check when you are updating files. However, be very careful...you may overwrite files that you need and you won't be warned again. To be safe, do not select this option. You will still have an opportunity later to overwrite the file when WinZip prompts you with the following screen:

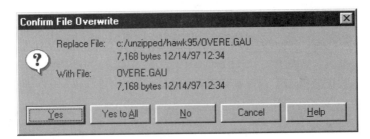

You may also choose whether filetype icons are displayed after the files are unzipped. Most users should have this box checked. Also notice the [Next>] button has become labeled [Unzip Now]. Click this when you are ready to unzip your file. After your files have been extracted, you may click [Next>] to work with another ZIP file or [Close] to exit. You will find the uncompressed files in the directory you specified.

Of course, if you have any questions while using the Wizard, just press [F1] to access WinZip's Help.

Using
WinZip
Help

WinZip for
Beginners

WinZip's detailed and easy-to-reach on-line help contribute to make this one of the most popular programs. Press [F1] anytime that WinZip is the active window for contextual help. For instance, if you press [F1] at the last step in the unzipping Wizard, WinZip will open a window explaining what each button in the Wizard will accomplish. From this window (or by pressing [F1] a second time, or by using the **Help** menu command in the WinZip Classic interface) you may navigate through WinZip's Help by the Contents, the Index or the Find feature.

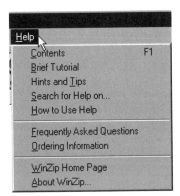

Click the "Contents" tab in the Help Topics dialog box to browse the Help file by topic. Double-click an entry to list the subjects within that category. Double-click one of these to further expand the directory tree or open that subject.

Click the "Index" tab to browse the contents of the Help file by keywords. Just enter the first few letters of the keyword(s) in the text field at the top or browse the list at the bottom. Double-click an entry in this list to display the full entry on that topic.

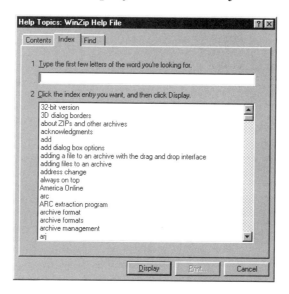

WinZip for Beginners

Click the "Find" tab to search for specific terms throughout the Help file. The first time you use this feature, WinZip will ask you to set the parameters for the search. For best results, select the "Maximize search capabilities" option, even though it will take a little longer to prepare.

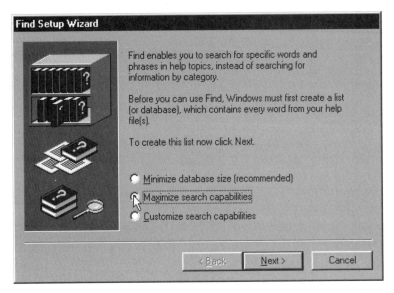

Each of these features uses a different approach to reach the same answers. Use whichever makes you most comfortable. The Help file addresses issues from double-clicking to installing optional add-on programs. You'll even find Help topics on how to use Help. All these entries can be printed out, so you may reference a hard copy while working on your computer.

You may also access Help from the Classic interface. We'll more fully explain the Classic interface in the next section, but since we're talking about Help here, we'll explore all the options you have to answer questions and discover new features. You can see the Classic interface by starting WinZip and clicking the [WinZip Classic] button. Click **Help**, the right-most menu bar command.

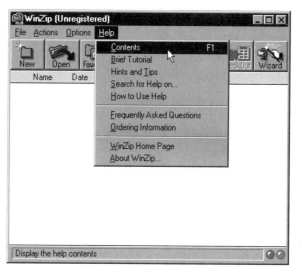

Clicking **Contents** (in the **Help** menu) offers the same Contents/ Index/Find pages we saw above.

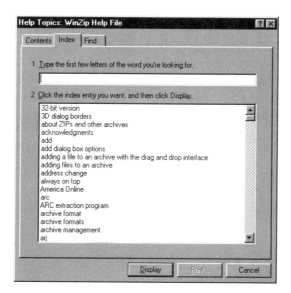

Below the **Contents** command is the **Brief Tutorial** command. This explores ten topics highlighting each of the main WinZip concepts and features, from viewing archives to creating custom configurations. You may either go directly to the topics that interest you (by clicking on that item) or follow the tutorial's sequence by clicking the Next link at the bottom of the page. This tutorial is an informative and easy way to familiarize yourself with the WinZip tools that you will most be using.

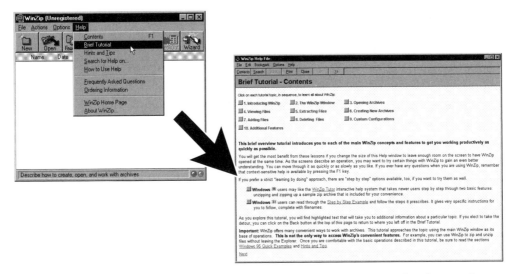

The next command in the **Help** menu is **Hints and Tips**. These explain how you can better use WinZip's features to save time, incorporate helper programs and more.

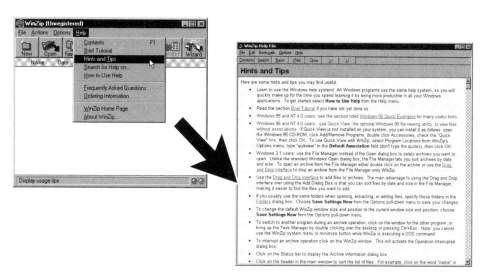

The **How to Use Help** command explains precisely that: how to get the most from these Help files. You'll learn to bookmark Help topics, insert comments and more so that your Help file can better assist you.

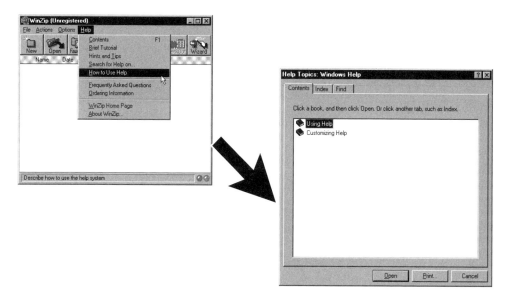

WinZip for Beginners

You may also access the **Frequently Asked Questions** file using this **Help** menu.

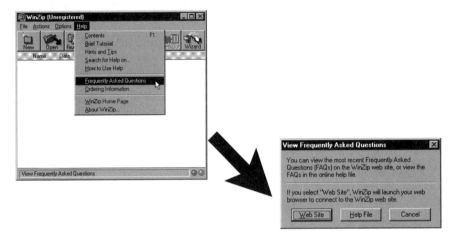

Frequently Asked Questions (FAQs) are just that: questions that have been addressed to WinZip's support staff many times. To avoid hearing them again (and again), these questions have been collected into a list for you to peruse, so you won't call with the same question.

These cover everything from "How do I get started?" to queries about spanning several floppy disks with a single ZIP file. You have the option of viewing the FAQs from the on-line Help file or at the Web site, where you'll find the most recent and complete questions and answers.

Selecting to view the Web site FAQs will launch your dialer and browser and take you to the WinZip Web site. If you don't have Web access or don't want to log on right now, view the Help file FAQs.

Ordering Information and **WinZip Homepage** are the next two items in the Help menu. The first explains how you can order a registered version of WinZip.

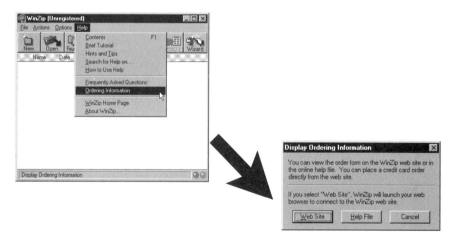

The second launches your Web dialer and browser and points to www.winzip.com, where you can learn about the latest updates, plans for the next release and more in-depth information about how and why to use WinZip.

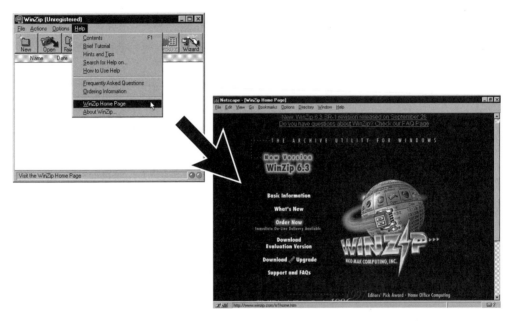

The last command in the **Help** menu is **About WinZip...**. It has important information concerning WinZip. First, you'll find your program's version number here. This tells you (and technical support personnel) with exactly what build of the program you are working. This window also has copyright and contact information (for the internet, Web, CompuServe and normal post). It also has buttons that summon ordering information, the user license (which you agree to by using the program), acknowledgments to those who helped create and improve WinZip, and buttons that lead to the WinZip homepage and FAQs.

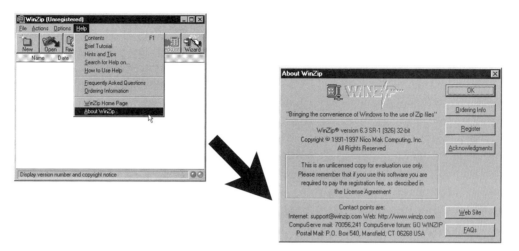

Support

So what do you do when you need help? If exploring the brief tutorial and the Help FAQs didn't answer your questions, the WinZip Web site has a wealth of information. The FAQs on the Web site will probably be more recent (and maybe larger) than the questions and answers in the Help file. WinZip's Web site also has a search feature. So if you don't see your question addressed in the FAQs, you can find any and all pages in the WinZip site that mention your topic. If, after all this, you still have an unanswered question, prepare to send an e-mail message to help@winzip.com.

Before you do, prepare answers to these questions:

* Can you (always, sometimes or never) reproduce this problem in the program?

* Does the error occur with all files, some files or just one file?

* What operating system (Win 3.x, Win95, Mac, etc.) are you using?

WinZip for Beginners

* What version of WinZip are you using? (See **Help | About WinZip...**)

* If there is an error message, exactly what does it say?

Having answers prepared for these questions will save you and a technical specialist time and frustration.

You have many options for getting help when using WinZip. Many dialog boxes have a question mark icon in the upper-right corner (see illustration to the right).

Click on this (your cursor will change to an arrow with a question mark) and then on another item in the box to receive an explanation of that item. The WinZip Web site (www.winzip.com) can answer most questions. If neither the Help file nor the Web site solves your dilemma, prepare answers to the questions above and send an e-mail to help@winzip.com, and a technician will quickly reply.

Chapter 5

Using WinZip Classic

WinZip for Beginners

The WinZip Wizard is incredibly easy to use. The trade off for this is that the Wizard is limited to unzipping files and installing programs. The WinZip Classic interface is only slightly more involved to use, but it accomplishes so much more. With the Classic interface one may unzip files and install programs, of course, but also view the contents of ZIP archives, create your own ZIP files, pack several files into a ZIP file and do even more. Once you are familiar with the Classic interface, you may never go back to the Wizard.

To use the Classic interface, launch WinZip and click the [WinZip Classic] button in the lower-left corner of the Wizard.

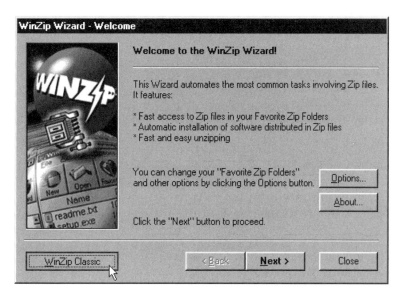

Return to the Wizard any time by clicking the right-most toolbar button labeled Wizard (see below right). You can also click **File | Wizard** in the menu bar (shown to the far right). Power users may opt to press ⌨Ctrl + ⌨W.

The Wizard is there for you if you want a quick and brainless avenue to unzipping and installing new ZIP files, but you probably won't need it once you are comfortable with WinZip Classic.

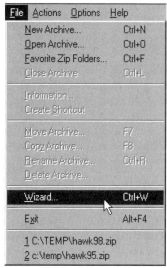

The Program Window

Before we begin using WinZip, let's take a moment to explore the program window.

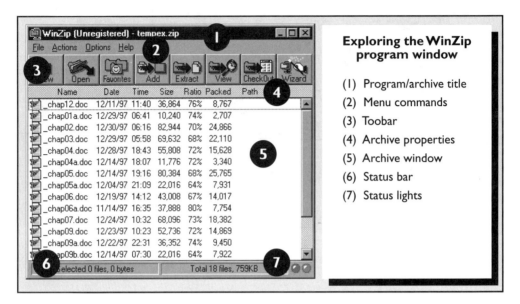

Exploring the WinZip program window

(1) Program/archive title
(2) Menu commands
(3) Toobar
(4) Archive properties
(5) Archive window
(6) Status bar
(7) Status lights

WinZip identifies itself and the active ZIP archive at the top of the program window **(1)**. TEMPEX.ZIP is the archive opened in this example.

Below this is the menu bar **(2)**, with a menu for **File**, **Actions**, **Options**, and **Help**. You may control every aspect of WinZip through these menu commands, from editing archives through setting your configuration preferences. Each command will be explained as we look into the action it performs. A complete description of each menu command's function can be found in the first appendix.

The toolbar **(3)** is underneath this, with easy-access buttons for commonly used features. These are alternatives to looking for commands in the menu bar.

The archive window **(4)(5) is** where you may look at the contents of a ZIP file.

Name	Date	Time	Size	Ratio	Packed	Path
_chap12.doc	12/11/97	11:40	36,864	76%	8,767	
_chap01a.doc	12/17/97	11:19	9,728	80%	1,914	
_chap02.doc	12/19/97	05:59	75,264	71%	21,626	
_chap03.doc	12/17/97	17:20	78,336	69%	24,173	
_chap04.doc	12/16/97	06:17	51,712	73%	13,743	
_chap04a.doc	12/14/97	18:07	11,776	72%	3,340	
_chap05.doc	12/14/97	19:16	80,384	68%	25,765	
_chap05a.doc	12/04/97	21:09	22,016	64%	7,931	
_chap06.doc	12/19/97	10:25	62,976	74%	16,545	
_chap06a.doc	11/14/97	16:35	37,888	80%	7,754	
_chap09.doc	12/18/97	21:45	49,152	69%	15,056	
_chap09a.doc	12/12/97	11:34	40,960	77%	9,429	
_chap09b.doc	12/14/97	07:30	22,016	64%	7,922	
_chap10.doc	12/13/97	21:03	33,792	73%	9,015	

The name and file type of each file in the archive is shown on the left. Next to this are the dates and times that each of the files was created. To the right of this are the files' sizes, before compression. The *Ratio* column lists the percentage by which the files shrank during compression—you can see in this example that the files' sizes were reduced between 64 and 80 percent. *Packed* tells how large the individual files are after compression.

You may sort the archived files by any of these columns. For example, to sort the files by name, simply click on *Name* at the top of the archive window. If you'd prefer to have them listed in the order in which they were created, click on *Date*. You may sort by any of the columns.

The status bar **(6)** is at the bottom of the program window. On the left you'll see the number and cumulative size of all the selected files in the open archive. On the right you'll find the total number of files in the archive and their cumulative unzipped size.

Selected 0 files, 0 bytes	Total 17 files, 720KB

Click once on the status bar to display information about this archive. This dialog box (also available through the **File | Information** menu command) displays the directory path of the current ZIP file, its name, size, compression percentage, and the date and time it was created.

In the lower-right corner of the WinZip program window are two status lights: a red and a green **(7)**. The red light indicates that WinZip is currently busy (extracting a file, for example). The green light says WinZip is not currently engaged and is ready for your next command.

Different Paths To The Same End

Another aspect of WinZip that has made it so popular is that you can use it how you want to use it. In other words, each goal you may have can be reached by several paths.

The menu commands offer complete control over your archives.

The most commonly used actions, such as creating a new archive and opening, viewing or extracting files, can also be performed by buttons in the toolbar.

Or, you may right-click on files. Right-clicking on a file in WinZip's archive window opens a menu identical to the **Actions** menu in the command bar.

If you prefer an icon-based, drag-and-drop interface, you can drop a ZIP archive into WinZip's archive window or onto the WinZip program icon to unzip that file. You may also use Drag-and-drop actions to open, add, print and view files. Drag a file from the archive window onto your printer's icon to print that file. Drag a file into the archive window to add it to the open archive. You may extract files by dragging them to a directory in Windows' Explorer. Dragging a file onto a program shortcut will use that program to open the file (the same occurs when a file is dragged from WinZip onto an open application window). For easy access to newly extracted files, you may drag them from WinZip onto the desktop.

You may also work with ZIP files without leaving Explorer. For example, you can extract the files within an archive by using the right mouse button to drag the ZIP from an Explorer window to any directory, and selecting *Extract to* from the context menu. You can create a new archive by right-clicking in Explorer and selecting **New | WinZip File**.

Open an archive in Explorer by simply double-clicking on it (or selecting it and clicking **File | Open**). You may add files to an archive by dragging them to a ZIP file in Explorer or on the desktop. Right-clicking on a file in Explorer also offers the option *Add to Zip*, which summons a dialog box similar to the Add button in WinZip's toolbar. Of course, WinZip also supports Win 95's long filenames and Universal Naming Convention.

However you use Windows, WinZip is ready to streamline into your preferred mode. You don't have to learn arcane or proprietary conventions to get the most out of WinZip. You can operate most of its features just as you already use your computer.

Chapter 6

Viewing The Contents Of A ZIP Archive

WinZip for Beginners

The first step in working with any ZIP file is discovering exactly what that ZIP contains. While WinZip can work with almost any file type with no input from you, you will find it very useful to know whether you are working with text, program or data files.

It's very easy to use WinZip to look inside compressed files, and there are several ways to do so. Each of the following methods can be used to open a zipped archive.

Explorer example #1

The simplest is to double-click the ZIP file in Explorer. This launches WinZip, which will display the contents of the archive. (See the illustration on the following page.)

Viewing The Contents Of A ZIP Archive

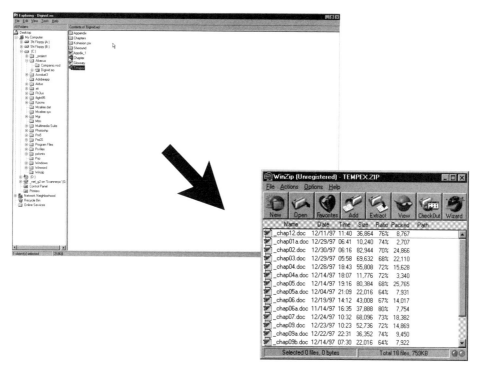

Explorer example #2

If you are using Explorer to locate your ZIP file, right-click the file and select **Open**. (This is effectively the same as selecting the archive and clicking **File | Open** in Explorer's menu bar.) This also launches WinZip and opens the archive. (See the illustration on the following page.)

WinZip for Beginners

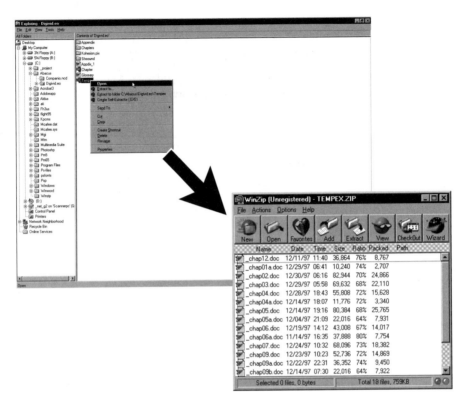

Click and drag

You may also click on the ZIP file and drag it onto WinZip's program icon or onto WinZip's archive window. (See illustration on the following page.)

Viewing The Contents Of A ZIP Archive

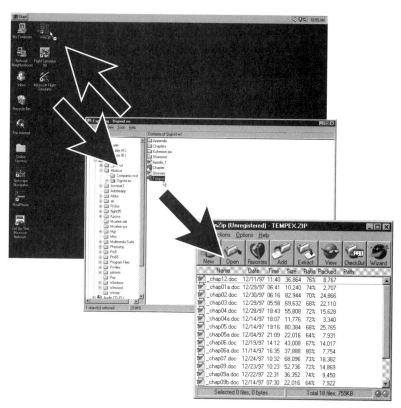

Click the Open button in WinZip's toolbar. Use the dialog box to select the file you wish to view and click (Open). (See the illustration on the following page.)

WinZip for Beginners

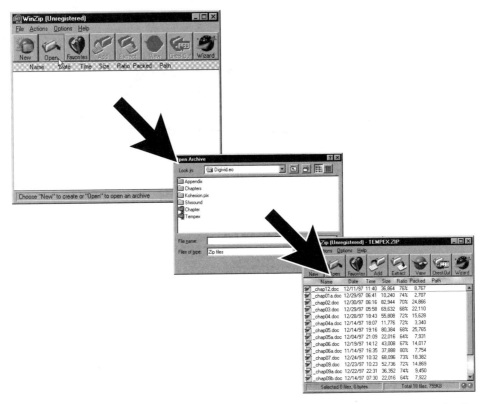

Selecting **File | Open Archive...** displays the same Open dialog. Locate your file, highlight it and click Open. (See the illustration on the following page.)

Viewing The Contents Of A ZIP Archive

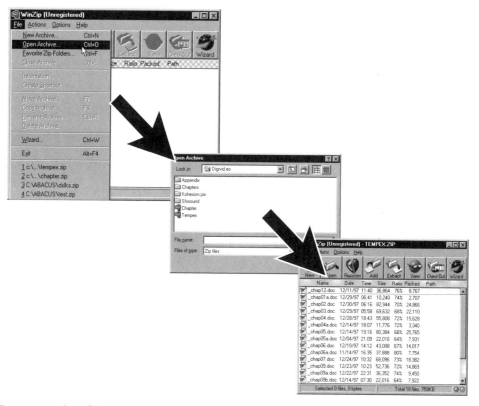

Viewing the files is an important step in unzipping a compressed file. After opening an archive, but before it is extracted, you should view the archive to be sure it contains what you expect. You should also read any text files included in the archive. These will often have important information about installing the new files, and may even tell you to what directory the archive should be extracted. Or if the archive holds images, you can preview them before you extract them into a directory on your hard drive.

You have several ways to view archive files. First you should identify which files you want to view. Files are listed on the left of the archive window by their names and file extensions. This three-letter extension indicates what type of file you have, for example, whether it is a picture or a text file. These two examples are types that will most often be viewed. Some files contain data needed by the program, and will never be viewed (if you try, you'll only see meaningless symbols and/or code). Others are program files. Attempting to view these by the following procedures will either run the program or do nothing at all. All these files can be easily identified by the three-letter file extension (see following table).

File type	Extensions
Image files	.bmp, .gif, .tif, .jpg, .msp and others
Text files	.txt, .wri, .doc, .rtf, READ.ME, READ.1st, and others
Program files	.exe, .bat, .com
Data files	.dat, .diz, .dot and many others

Perhaps the simplest way to view a file within an archive is to double-click it in the archive window.

Alternatively, select the file and click the View button. This displays the View dialog box. Then select the program associated with this type of file (named in parentheses), the WinZip internal ASCII text viewer or browse your way to another program for viewing. Click [View] after you have selected the program which will display the file.

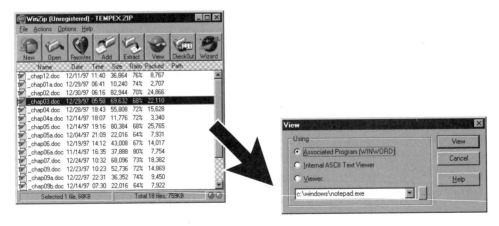

Viewing The Contents Of A ZIP Archive

You can also right-click on the file you wish to view and select **View...** from the context menu. This also brings the View dialog box.

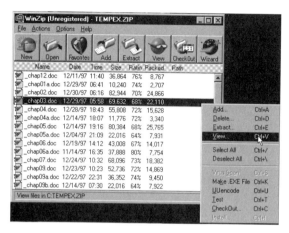

Selecting the file and clicking **Actions | View...** does the same thing.

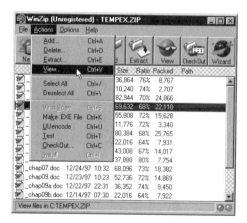

You may also drag the file to the proper program's icon. For example, I can drag a .DOC file from an archive and drop it onto the Word icon on my desktop to view that file. (Note that if you drag a word processor file from an archive onto an already-open document in your word processor, the new document will be inserted into the open document at the point you drop it.)

If you modify the file you are viewing (such as editing a document), WinZip will ask you if you want to add the modified file to the ZIP, replacing the original version.

Important Note

Nico Mak Computing recommends you install the QuickView utility from the Windows 95 CD-ROM to handle files that are not associated with another program. QuickView easily displays graphic, spreadsheet and word processor files that were created with many programs. Associating programs with file-types will be explained later.

Chapter 7

Unzipping

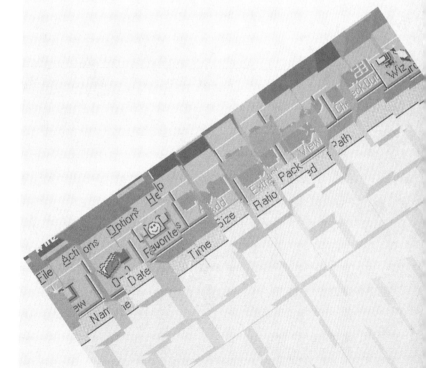

WinZip for Beginners

After viewing the contents of a ZIP file, you must unzip (or extract, or decompress, or unpack) the file before you can make use of it. Again, there are several ways to achieve this.

To unzip an archive using WinZip's program window, first you must open the archive. This is explained at the start of Chapter Six.

Once the file is opened in WinZip's archive window, you have three ways to extract it, plus two more using Windows Explorer. First, if you don't want to extract all the files in the ZIP, hold down the Ctrl key and click each of the files you want to unzip. Then follow these steps:

    1. Click **Actions | Extract...** in WinZip's menu bar.

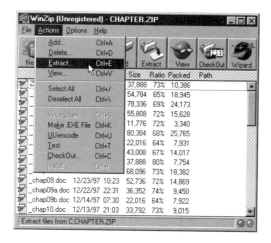

or

2. Click the Extract button in WinZip's toolbar.

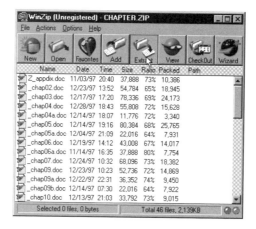

or

3. Right-click the selected file(s) and choose **Extract...** from the context menu.

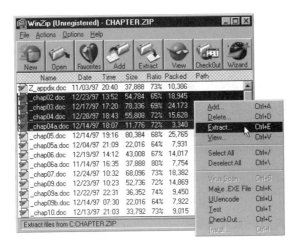

Each of these methods summons the Extract dialog box.

Now decide to where you want the selected files unzipped. You may type this path into the "Extract to:" field or browse in the "Folders/Drives:" window. If you want to place the archive files into a new directory, specify the path to that directory and click the New Folder... button.

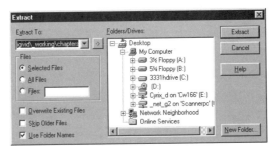

On the left of the Extract dialog box you'll see a few more options. In the "Files" area you can set WinZip to extract all the files in the archive, only selected files, or specify precisely which files you wish to unpack in the entry field. DOS wildcard characters, like the asterisk '*', are accepted.

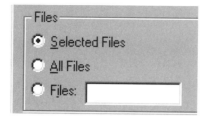

Placing a check in the box next to "Overwrite Existing Files" allows WinZip to replace files that have the same names as new ones you are extracting without prompting you for permission.

Marking the box next to "Skip Older Files" will not extract files that have the same name but earlier dates relative to files already on your computer.

If you mark "Use Folder Names," WinZip will recreate the directory paths for the archive files, if any were specified when the ZIP file was created. For example, the file MYTEXT.TXT may be marked to go into a directory titled MYDOCS. If you extract it to C:\TEMP with this option, the text file will be extracted to C:\TEMP\MYDOCS. If you extract it to C:\TEMP without this option, MYTEXT.TXT will be put into C:\TEMP.

When you have identified the destination directory and set your desired options, click the [Extract] button.

Windows Explorer offers two more ways to extract ZIP files:

1. Using the right-mouse button, click and drag a ZIP file to a directory in Explorer or onto the desktop. This unzips the archive into that directory.

2. You may also right-click a ZIP file in Explorer and select **Extract to...** from the context menu. This opens the Extract dialog box.

You have great control over unzipping compressed files after moving beyond the WinZip Wizard. The Classic interface is so easy to use because it offers so many ways to unzip files. Whether using the menu commands, toolbars, context menus or Explorer, you are only a few mouse clicks away from using the files in any zipped archive.

Zipping

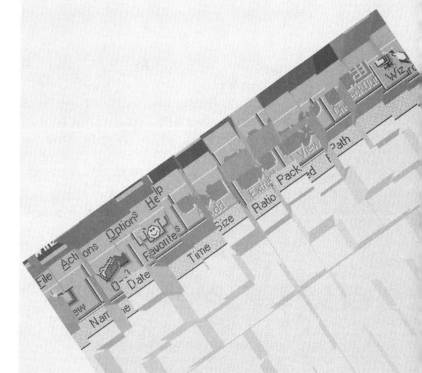

WinZip for
Beginners

U nzipping allows you to access many files from the internet and elsewhere. But if you only use WinZip for unzipping, you're missing some of its most useful applications. This chapter teaches you to use WinZip to create your own ZIPs, which can organize your files while saving time and disk space.

Like other WinZip functions, zipping is very easy and there are a number of routes to accomplish it. The first step is to create a new archive. You have at least six ways to do this:

1. In WinZip, select **File | New Archive...** from the menu bar.

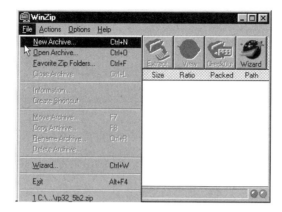

or

2. Click the New button in WinZip's toolbar.

or

3. Select the file(s) you wish to zip in Explorer and drag onto WinZip's program window. Click the [New...] button in the Add dialog box.

or

4. Right-click on the file(s) in Explorer and select **Add to Zip** from the context menu. Click the [New...] button in the Add dialog box.

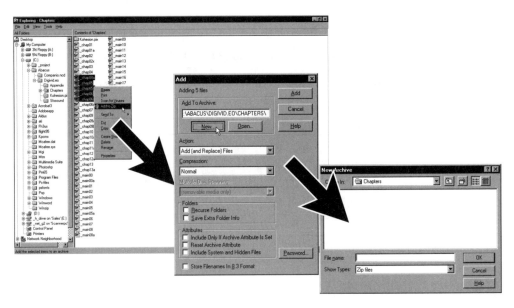

or

5. Select the file(s) in Explorer and click **File | Add to Zip** in Explorer's menu bar. Click (New...) in the Add dialog box.

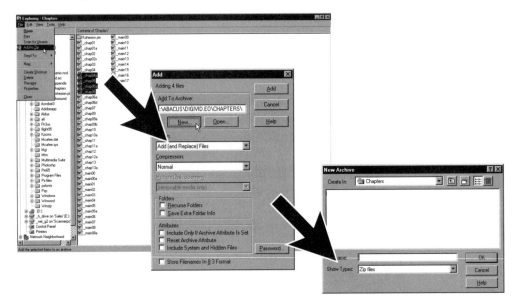

or

6. In Explorer's menu bar, click **File | New | WinZip File**.

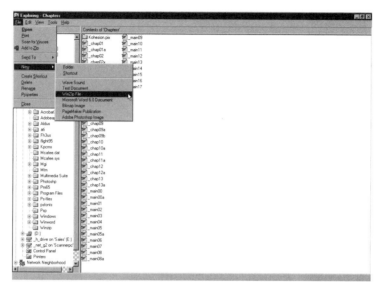

The last of these methods creates an untitled ZIP file in the active directory. After titling the file, you'll need to add the files you wish to compress, which we'll explain in a moment.

Using the New Archive dialog box

The rest of these bring up the New Archive dialog box.

WinZip for Beginners

Select the directory where you wish the new archive to be created and type a name for it in the "File name:" field. If the "Add Dialog" check box is marked, the Add dialog box appears when you click ⌐OK⌐.

Now you are ready to pack files into your newly created ZIP file. Select the file you want to zip by locating the proper directory in the "Add from:" field and clicking on the file. The selected file should appear in the "File name:" field.

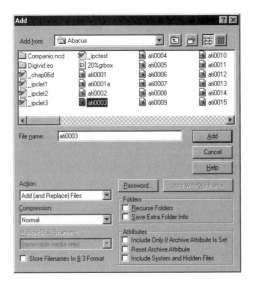

The bottom of this dialog box has several options you may wish to apply to your new archive before you click Add.

You have four options for exactly what "Action:" will be taken on the specified file. In most cases, you'll select "Add (and Replace) Files," which adds the specified file to the archive. 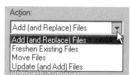 "Move Files" operates the same as "Add...," but the file is deleted from disk after being added to the ZIP. Effectively, this option moves the file from your hard disk into the archive. "Freshen Existing Files" updates a file already in the archive that matches the file specified in this dialog box. Selecting "Update (and Add) Files" behaves the same as "Freshen...," but also adds any selected files which aren't already in the archive.

You may also select your preferred level of "Compression:" as "Maximum", "Normal", "Fast", "Superfast" or "None". Faster compression usually creates a larger archive, and selecting "None" defeats the purpose of 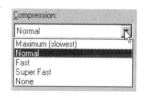 zipping unless you are only using it to organize files.

"Multiple Disk Spanning" is only available when your new ZIP archive is located on removable media, such as floppy disks. Disk spanning is explained in the next chapter.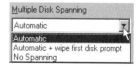

Mark the check box next to "Store Filenames in 8.3 Format" if you want WinZip to rename files with long names according to DOS file naming conventions (i.e., a maximum of eight characters plus a three-letter filetype extension, such as 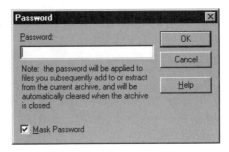 12345678.123). This is important if anyone will be working with the files in Windows 3.x or DOS.

You may protect your archived files from prying eyes with a password. If you wish to do so, just click the [Password...] button. The "Mask Password" option hides password characters as you type them. If you enable this you'll be asked to reenter the password for confirmation. However, please read the Help topic *Password Security* before using passwords to lock your archives.

WinZip also allows you to use wildcard characters to specify which file(s) to add to the archive. WinZip recognizes the question mark '?' and asterisk '*' as wildcards. These can be substituted for other text characters. For example, if you wanted to add the ONE.TXT, TWO.TXT and THREE.TXT files to your archive, you could simply enter *.TXT as the filename, and all .TXT files in the selected directory would be included. This is also useful if you aren't sure how a file's name is spelled ("br*an" would bring "brian" and "bryan"), desire word variants ("scien*" brings "science" and "scientist"), or if you want to specify a group of files with the same name but different file types (ABC.TXT, ABC.EXE and ABC.DAT are equivalent to ABC.*). To use this feature, enter your wildcard filenames in the filename field and click the [Add With Wildcards] button instead of the [Add] button.

You also have control over how WinZip handles folders in your archive. Marking the check box next to "Recurse Folders" commands WinZip to collect files from all the folders within the folder you have identified. This makes it easy to back up all files underneath the directory containing the specified file, no matter how deeply nested they may be. To restore folders added with this option, be sure to select the "Use Folder Names" option in the Extract dialog box, mentioned in chapter seven. WinZip automatically saves path information for files in subfolders of the open folder. Selecting "Save Extra Folder Info" stores folder path information from the *Add Files From:* edit field. If you select this option, WinZip will extract the files into the same directory structure from which the files were copied, relative to the root directory. If this option is not marked, path information is saved relative to (but not including) the current open folder.

Many computer files have assigned attributes. You can check a file's attributes by right-clicking the file in Explorer and selecting **Properties** from the context menu. The file attributes are at the bottom of the Properties box. In the bottom, right corner of the WinZip Add dialog box you may control how WinZip handles attributed files. Selecting "Include Only If Archive Attribute Is Set" excludes files that have not been assigned attributes. "Reset Archive Attributes" turns off a file's attributes after it is added to the ZIP. Marking the box next to "Include System and Hidden Files" adds files marked as Hidden or System to the archive (these types of files are omitted by default).

When you have finished selecting the Add options, click the `Add` button to incorporate the specified files into the new archive (click `Add With Wildcards` if you have specified files with wildcard characters).

Adding files to an archive

Once you are working with ZIPs, you'll soon need to add files to newly created archives or to older ZIP files. This is very easy to do. In Windows Explorer you can add files to an archive by simply dragging them onto a ZIP. Alternatively, you may right-click on the file(s) you wish to add to the archive and select **Add to ZIP** from the context menu. This opens a variation on WinZip's Add dialog box.

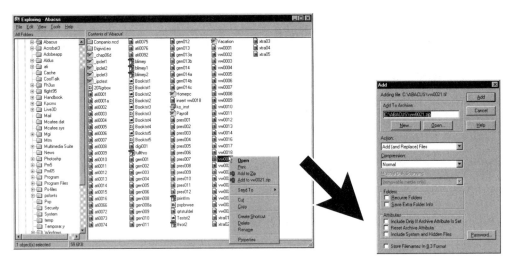

You may also drag files from anywhere and drop them into an opened archive in WinZip's archive window. Clicking the Add button or selecting **Action I Add...** from the menu commands also opens the Add dialog box, where you may specify the files you wish to include and which options should be in effect.

You may repeatedly add as many files as you wish to an archive. You can add as many files as you want from within a directory. To add files from multiple directories, you'll have to add them one directory at a time. For instance, when using the Add dialog box, select files from the Windows directory and click [Add], then select files from the Temp directory and click [Add].

All types of files can be zipped. This is an easy way to organize files while conserving disk space, and makes transferring files much quicker, whether across a local network, from one hard disk to another or sending files around the internet.

Chapter 9

Disk Spanning

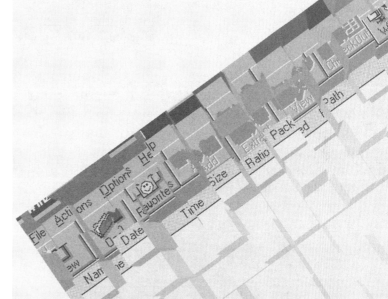

WinZip for Beginners

Sending ZIP files of almost any size across a computer network is easy and convenient. But what happens when you want to move files to a computer that isn't on a network? That's when floppy disks assert their usefulness—and their limits. A conventional floppy disk can hold 1.44 megabytes of computer information. WinZip will substantially reduce the size of files that are zipped, but many archives will still be larger than a single floppy can hold. This would be a serious limitation for most programs, but not for WinZip. WinZip lets you create compressed archives that span multiple disks. This means that you can create an archive of any size on a floppy disk (or other removable storage media), and WinZip will prompt you to insert another disk when the first one fills. It will continue prompting you for new disks until the entire ZIP file has been created on as many disks as are needed.

First copy each file you want zipped into a temporary directory. All the files to be in this archive must come from the same directory— files can not be added to or removed from archives that span multiple diskettes. These files can be deleted after the archive is created. (If all the files for this new archive already share the same directory, you may skip this step.)

Second, prepare a few more floppy disks than you think you'll need (you don't want to interrupt the zipping process to format one more disk). The disks need to be formatted, and you may delete any information on them now or let WinZip do that as it writes to the disks. (It is not absolutely necessary to remove data from the disks, as WinZip can use only the free disk space, but you will consequently use more disks. At the prices floppies sell for today, it is easy and affordable to buy new disks if you are already using all the floppies you own.) One may usually expect that zipping will reduce the collected files' sizes by about fifty percent.

Insert one of the prepared floppies into the floppy drive.

Create a new archive. (Chapter eight illustrates each of the ways this can be done. This example will show only one.)

* Click New in WinZip's toolbar.

* Select "3$^1/_2$ Floppy [A:]" in the *Create In:* field.

* Enter a name for the new archive.

* Be sure the "Add Dialog" check box is marked and click OK.

* Select the files you want to zip. (If every file in a directory is desired, select that directory in the *Add from:* field and leave the default "*.*" as the file name.)

* Select "Add (and Replace) Files" as the action.

* Select the preferred level of compression.

* You have three choices as Multiple Disk Spanning options: Automatic, Automatic plus Wipe First Disk, and No Spanning. The first prompts you to insert a new disk as each fills. The second does the same, plus erases any files in the first disk before writing to it. The last will force a disk-full error when the first disk fills up. Do not select this last option if you are planning on spanning disks with this archive.

* Select the other options according to your preferences.

* When you are ready, click [Add] (or [Add With Wildcards]).

WinZip will begin creating the archive on the floppy disk in drive A:. When ready, WinZip will prompt you to insert the next disk. Remember to label the disks as they finish so you can identify Disk One from Disk Two, etc. Highlight the box beside "Erase any existing files on the new disk before continuing" to remove old files from the floppy before WinZip continues archiving. Click [OK] after you have inserted the next disk. WinZip will continue to prompt you for new disks until the archive is complete. You can monitor the progress of the operation in WinZip's status bar, at the bottom of the WinZip program window.

Unzipping spanned archives

Unzipping spanned archives is almost identical to unpacking other ZIPs. Place the last disk of the spanned set into the floppy drive and view it like any other archive. When you are ready to extract it, you may do so just as you would another archive. The only difference is that WinZip will prompt you for the first disk of the set, and then each subsequent disk as WinZip needs them.

Spanning disks is very useful if you need to get files from one computer to another when those machines are not connected by a network. As you can see, it is not difficult and can be very useful.

Chapter 10

Self-extracting Files

WinZip for Beginners

WinZip makes it easy to share files. But what happens when you want to send a ZIP to someone who isn't using WinZip? You use WinZip to create a self-extracting .EXE file. These are compressed archives that have a small piece of WinZip's program (less than 12K) included in the archive. Users run these .EXE files just like any other program. When they do so, the small piece of WinZip extracts the compressed files, then deletes itself, leaving the uncompressed archive. These are ideal for sending to friends or colleagues who may be unfamiliar with zipping programs.

To create a self-extracting ZIP, first create a ZIP archive as you normally would (see chapter eight). Once you have the files zipped, Open the archive in WinZip and select **Actions | Make .EXE** from WinZip's menu bar. This runs the WinZip Self-Extractor Personal Edition, which displays a dialog to set the default unzipping options.

The *Create Self Extracting ZIP From:* field shows the currently open WinZip archive. If this is not the ZIP you wish to convert to a self-extracting file, click the browse button and select the file you wish to convert.

In the next box down you may select the default directory to where the file will be unzipped. If no directory is specified, WinZip defaults to the directory specified as TEMP on the user's machine.

Below this, you determine whether this .EXE file will be a 16- or 32-bit program. 16-bit programs can run on any PC-type computer, while 32-bit programs require an interface such as Windows 95 or NT. 32-bit files can have long filenames; 16-bit files must be in the DOS 8.3 format.

If you make this a 16-bit application, you also have the option of using "CTL3D.DLL For 3D Effects If Available" when the program is extracted. CTL3D.DLL generates 3-d effects, such as clickable buttons. This file is used by many programs, so many computers will have it.

The last option determines whether the "Overwrite by default" option is enabled or not by default in the self-extractor's unzipping dialog. When this option is active, WinZip will overwrite existing files that have the same name as files being extracted without prompting the user for permission. The end user can change these options during unzipping.

When you have configured the self-extracting options, click [Make .EXE].

Another dialog will open asking if you wish to test the new archive. Click [Yes].

Click [Close] in the dialog box when you are finished. Be sure to test any self-extracting archives you create before you distribute them. This may be done when the archive is created, or later by opening the ZIP in WinZip and selecting **Actions | Test** from the command bar.

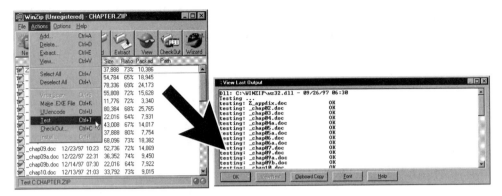

Users who want still more control over self-extracting archives should consider the WinZip Self Extractor 2.1. This is a separate program ($49), designed for users who will be using the self-extractor for larger scale file distribution. It does everything the Personal Edition does plus more: automates and customizes software installation, supports InstallShield 3.0 setup, runs a command after unzipping, offers a Wizard interface, displays multiple languages and more.

Unzipping Self-extracting files

To decompress a self-extracting file, simply run it like any other program (by double-clicking or using **Start | Run...**, as examples). This launches the self-extractor's unzip dialog box, where users may accept the defaults set by the person who created the archive or select their preferred destination directory and options.

Clicking [Unzip] extracts the files to the specified directory. Clicking [Run WinZip] opens the archive in WinZip, if that is on the user's computer. [About] displays copyright and contact information.

Self-extracting files are only slightly larger than normal ZIPs. These are the perfect solution when you need to compress files for someone who may not be familiar with ZIP files. The user doesn't even need to know that the file is compressed. He or she runs it like any other program, and WinZip does the rest.

Chapter 11

Install/Try /Uninstall

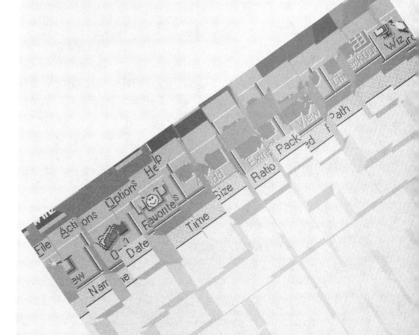

WinZip for Beginners

WinZip does more than just zip and unzip compressed archives. It can also help you load new programs and maintain a "clean" computer system. When you install a new program onto your computer, it often makes changes to your system so it will run properly. If you later remove this program manually, files associated with this program may be scattered throughout your computer. These can be very difficult to identify and remove on your own. WinZip's Install/Try/Uninstall feature makes it easy to install and remove software in ZIP files.

If you have a zipped archive that contains a SETUP or INSTALL program, WinZip can install the new software for you. When it does so, WinZip keeps track of all the changes the installation program makes to your computer. And if, after trying the new program, you decide you don't want it, you may use WinZip to uninstall it. WinZip then removes the program and, based on the information recorded during installation, restores your computer to the way it was before the installation. This means you won't have to worry about leftover registry keys, INI files, icons and other hard-to-reach files occupying space on your computer.

The Install/Try/Uninstall feature is (at this moment) only available for the Windows 3.1 and Windows for Workgroups (16-bit) version of WinZip. The Windows 95 and NT (32-bit) version of WinZip can install programs for you, but can not perform uninstalls. Windows 95/NT users may download a beta add-on version of the uninstall feature from the WinZip Web site (www.winzip.com).

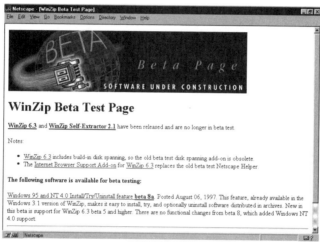

Downloading a beta add-on version of the uninstall feature.

This is a beta (test) edition, and users should be comfortable using beta software (and have system backups) before installing this add-on. Once the final kinks are worked out, this feature will be added to the next edition of WinZip. Windows 3.1 users, however, can take advantage of this right now.

Like other features of WinZip, Install/Try/Uninstall is very easy to use. First you need a zipped installation program. For example, the Web holds many computer game demonstrations. These are almost always compressed with an install program, which makes them an ideal example. Www.gamecenter.com, www.happypuppy.com, www.filez.com and www.download.com are just a few of the sites to check out if you want to download a file to experiment with this feature. You may have other archives on your computer that can be used, also.

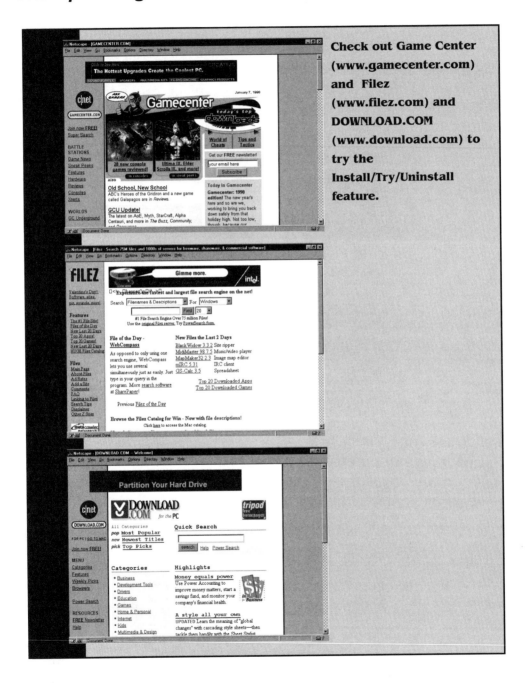

Check out Game Center (www.gamecenter.com) and Filez (www.filez.com) and DOWNLOAD.COM (www.download.com) to try the Install/Try/Uninstall feature.

First, open the archive in WinZip just as you would any other. To use Install/Try/Uninstall the archive must contain an executable file (*.EXE) that has "install" or "setup" in the filename, and this file must not contain folder information. Also, the entire program must be in one archive—Install/Try/Uninstall will not work if the program is parceled into several archives.

If the ZIP meets these requirements, the next step is to click the (Install)toolbar button or select **Actions | Install...** from the menu commands.

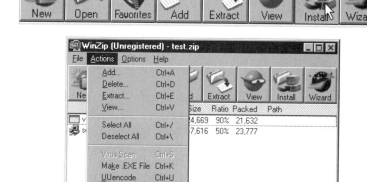

The Install dialog box offers two choices.

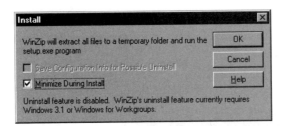

You must mark the "Save Configuration Information for Possible Uninstall" checkbox if you want to be able to uninstall the program with WinZip. (This option is disabled under Windows 95/NT.) Marking the "Minimize During Installation" checkbox minimizes the WinZip window during the installation process. Click OK to begin installing. WinZip will extract the archive to a temporary directory and run

Important Note

WinZip assumes all configuration changes made between installation and uninstallation have been made by the installation program. For example, if you switch to a word processor during the installation and save a document, WinZip assumes that this document is part of the installation, and will offer to remove it during uninstall. Nico Mak Computing, Inc., strongly suggests that you do not run any programs other than those related to the program you are installing until you have decided whether to uninstall.

the setup routine which installs the program. Do not close WinZip until you are sure you do not want to remove the program; WinZip does not save install/uninstall information across sessions.

After installation is finished, and after you've evaluated the newly installed program, return to WinZip. If you want to keep the program, choose the "No Uninstall Wanted" radio button. Select the "View Configuration Options for Possible Uninstall" button to display the Uninstall dialog box. Click OK.

The Uninstall dialog box lists the items that WinZip can remove. WinZip's uninstall feature can remove program groups and icons, folders and files created by the installation program, and can restore AUTOEXEC.BAT, CONFIG.SYS, REG.DAT and *.INI files in the Windows directory that were changed by the installation. Because it is a Windows program, WinZip is unable to notice files or folders the installation program created in DOS.

By default, each item in the Uninstall list is marked for removal. Click on an item to deselect it. Clicking on an item also displays information about it at the bottom of the dialog window. You may wish to click the

Important Note

If a program adds an uninstall routine to Windows's Add/Remove Programs applet, WinZip offers to run the Remove Programs feature, which helps uninstall any leftover changes to your system.

[Report...] button to save uninstallation information (such as what files are where) as a text file. This can be very helpful if a manual uninstall is required later. [Help] explains the options and buttons in the Uninstall dialog. You may click [Select All] to mark every file listed for removal. [Cancel] aborts the uninstallation. If there are configuration changes that WinZip's Uninstall can't restore, clicking [Caution...] will explain these. Click [Uninstall] to begin removing the program from your computer.

WinZip is more than just a zipping/unzipping utility. The Install/Try/Uninstall feature, for example, offers easy installation and removal of programs, letting you test new software and then remove it from your system without orphan INI and registry files haunting your computer.

Chapter 12

CheckOut

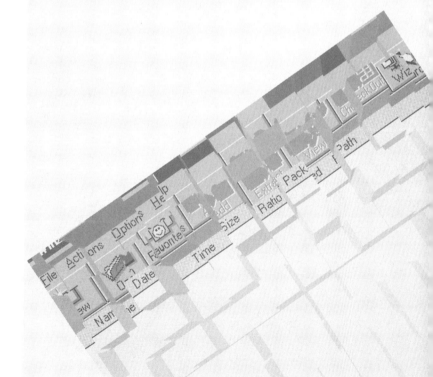

WinZip for Beginners

You know how to open an archive in WinZip to see what's inside. But sometimes a list of strange filenames doesn't tell you very much about what that ZIP contains. When you want to know more about a zipped file's contents, use WinZip's CheckOut feature to learn about the files inside an archive. This feature extracts the archive into a temporary folder and creates an icon for each file in the archive. You may then view or run these files. When you are done with them, WinZip will offer to remove the temporary files.

Open the archive in WinZip. Now click the CheckOut button in the toolbar or select **Actions | CheckOut...** from the menu bar. Both methods are shown in the illustrations on the right.

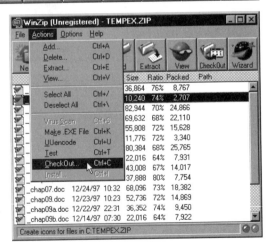

Both of these actions open the CheckOut dialog box. The *"Folder:"* edit field specifies the temporary folder where the files will be extracted. The default folder is determined by the "CheckOut Base Folder" entry in the Folders dialog box, under the **Options** menu (which is explained in the next section).

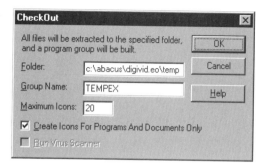

You may enter any path here, if you don't want to extract to the default directory. If you specify a folder that already exists, WinZip will ask for permission to delete the contents of that folder before extracting the archive. This ensures that the folder will only contain files from the archive you are checking out.

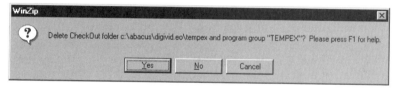

The *"Group Name:"* field shows the name that will be assigned to the program group. You may enter another name if you don't wish to use the default. If a program group with the name you specify already exists, WinZip will ask permission to delete its contents. Again, this ensures that only items from the current archive will appear in the program group.

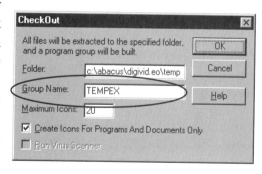

If you don't specify otherwise, WinZip will create an icon for every file in the archive. It can not, however, create more than 50 icons in a program group. You may further limit the number of icons WinZip creates by entering the desired number in the *Maximum Icons:* field.

You have more control over the program group icons with the "Create Icons For Programs and Documents Only" check box. If this option is marked, icons will only be created for .EXE files, files that have a Windows association, and files with names beginning "READ" (such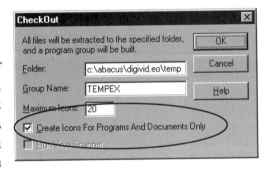

as README.TXT, READ.1ST, etc.). This is a good option to enable because it creates icons for files you can use and not for others that are simple data files, etc.

Lastly, selecting "Run Virus Scanner" will run an anti-virus program to check the archive's files before extracting them. This option is disabled if no scanning program is listed in the Program Locations window (explained in the next section).

Clicking [Help] explains the CheckOut feature and the dialog options. [Cancel] aborts the operation. Click [OK] to continue.

After you click [OK], WinZip will create the temporary folder (if necessary), extract the files, run the virus scanner and create the program group with the appropriate icons. If the virus scanner detects any problems, the CheckOut operation is aborted and messages from the anti-virus program are displayed.

You can now view the contents of the archive in the program group. Each file in the archive is depicted as an icon (unless you selected the "Create Icons For Programs and Documents Only" option, in which case only programs and associated files have icons). Double-clicking on the icon of a program will run that program. If a file has an association, double-clicking it will open that file in the associated program. If the file is not associated with a program, WinZip's Default Association program (specified in the Program Locations dialog box (explained soon)) attempts to display the file when you double-click its icon.

The CheckOut feature is a companion to the Install/Try/Uninstall feature. While the latter is useful for working with archives containing an installation routine, CheckOut provides the same service for other archives. CheckOut lets you unzip and examine the contents of archives, and makes it very easy to remove the extracted files (and their directory). If you decide that you want to keep the extracted files where they are, just click No when WinZip asks if you want to delete the temporary folder and its contents.

Chapter 13

Using WinZip With Other Programs

WinZip for Beginners

You can increase the power of WinZip by linking it to other programs, such as virus scanners or Web browsers. Associating WinZip with other programs lets you use the abilities of each without having to manually load each program and switch back and forth between them. WinZip can call upon certain programs as you need them, and close them after they have finished.

You make the associations to these programs in the Program Locations dialog box, which you'll find by clicking **Options | Program Locations...**

Using WinZip With Other Programs

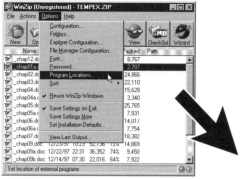

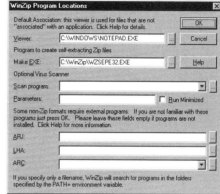

Viewer

The first entry in the Program Locations box shows the default

viewer WinZip uses to open a file if another program is not already associated with the file. This example uses Windows's Notepad text viewer to display unfamiliar files.

If you have installed the QuickView utility from the Windows 95 or Windows NT CD-ROM, WinZip will use QuickView as the viewer program. WinZip also looks for several other viewing programs on your system. If it doesn't find any of these (see sidebar), it defaults to Notepad, since this is on all 32-bit Windows systems.

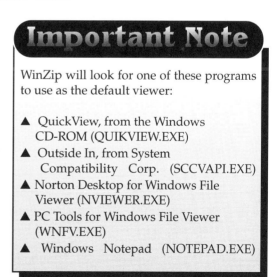

Important Note

WinZip will look for one of these programs to use as the default viewer:

▲ QuickView, from the Windows CD-ROM (QUIKVIEW.EXE)

▲ Outside In, from System Compatibility Corp. (SCCVAPI.EXE)

▲ Norton Desktop for Windows File Viewer (NVIEWER.EXE)

▲ PC Tools for Windows File Viewer (WNFV.EXE)

▲ Windows Notepad (NOTEPAD.EXE)

Make EXE

Listed next is the program that WinZip uses to create

self-extracting archives. Usually this is the WinZip Self-Extractor Personal Edition (WZSEPE*.EXE). If you have purchased and installed the more powerful WinZip Self-Extractor, then it should be listed here.

Scan Program

The next field displays the anti-virus scanner used to protect your computer. WinZip recognizes 14 anti-virus programs, including scanners from McAfee Associates, Norton, Central Point and Dr. Solomon.

During installation WinZip identifies the anti-virus software on your computer. If it successfully recognizes it, you'll see your A-V program listed in the Scan Program edit field. If you have anti-virus software installed on your computer but WinZip didn't find it, click the arrow on the right of the edit field. If your A-V program is in the drop list, select it. If your A-V program isn't listed, don't worry. That just means WinZip wasn't designed to look for that program.

To use your A-V program, enter its full path (i.e., drive:\directory\program) in the edit field. To use WinZip with a Windows-based scanner, be sure that the virus scanner reports suspected infections by displaying a dialog box; if the scanner only records virus information to a report file, WinZip won't know when it finds a problem.

If your virus scanner is DOS-based, be sure that it either can be run minimized or issues a prompt when a virus is found (again, you and WinZip won't know there is an infection otherwise). The Virus Scanner Configuration Help topic has important tips if you need to enter your scanner manually.

WinZip also sets command parameters for the scanning program. These provide instructions the scanning program will use to find viruses and notify you of the results. If WinZip sets these for you, it is best not to change them. If not, you can find the recommended parameters for most scanners in the Virus Scanner Configuration Help topic. (Note: the default parameters supplied by WinZip work properly with the scanners that were tested. If more recent editions of a scanning program change the parameters used by earlier versions, WinZip's default parameters may no longer work. For example, McAfee's SCAN 2.1 parameters are incompatible with earlier versions of SCAN; this version replaced the "/A" switch with "/ALL.")

WinZip and an anti-virus program can scan archives for viruses before they can infect your system. You may start your virus hunting software from within WinZip by opening an archive and selecting **Actions | Virus Scan** from the menu bar.

You may also activate it during a CheckOut operation by enabling the "Run Virus Scanner" option in the CheckOut dialog box. When you use the first method, WinZip creates a temporary directory, extracts the active archive to that directory, runs the scanning program against the extracted files, deletes the files and their directory, and then displays the results of the scan.

Virus Scanners Supported By WinZip 6.3			
Product Name	Vendor Name	Web Page	
Norton Anti Virus	Symantec	http//www.symantec.com	
Norton Anti Virus	Symantec	http//www.symantec.com	
Norton Anti Virus	Symantec	http//www.symantec.com	
Norton Anti Virus	Symantec	http//www.symantec.com	
McAfee Virus Scan	McAfee	http//www.mcafee.com	
McAfee Virus Scan	McAfee	http//www.mcafee.com	
McAfee Virus Scan	McAfee	http//www.mcafee.com	
Thunder BYTE Anti Virus	EsaSS B.V.	http//www.thunderbyte.nl	
Dr. Solomon's FindVirus	Dr. Solomon's Software	http//www.drsolomon.com	
F-PROT	FinnishSoftwareIntl.	Various ftp & BBSSites	
NortonDesktopFor Windows(Anti Virus)	Symantec	http//www.symantec.com	
Central Point PC Tools for Windows (AntiVirus)	Symantec	http//www.symantec.com	
Central Point Desktop for Windows (AntiVirus)	Symantec	http//www.symantec.com	
Central PointAnti-Virus	Symantec	http//www.symantec.com	
MicrosoftAnti Virus	Microsoft	http//www.microsoft.com	
McAfee Virus Scan	McAfee	http//www.mcafee.com	
Integrity Master	Stiller Research	http//www.stiller.com	

Other Compression Formats

ZIP is the most popular compression format for computer data, but it isn't the only one that is (or has been) used. As computers evolve, so do the tools we use with them, and data compression programs are no exception. As you hunt through the internet, you

Filename	Parameters	Iconized	Version	OS
NAV.EXE	*.* /m- /s	false	2.0	Win 3.1
NAVW32.EXE	*.* /s	false	4.0	Win 95
NAVWNT.EXE	*.* /s	false	4.0	NT
NAVW.EXE	*.* /s	false	4.0	Win 3.1
SCAN95.EXE	*.* /autoscan /nosplash	false	3.1.4	Win 95
SCAN32.EXE	%d /autoscan /nosplash	false	3.0.3	NT
SCAN.EXE	/nomem *.* /all /sub /report %f	true	3.1.2	Win 3.1
TBSCAN.EXE	*.* ln=%f lo nb nm	false	8.03a	Win95/ NT MS- DOS*
WFINDVIR.EXE	*.*	true	7.78	Win 3.1
FPROT.EXE	*.* /NOBOOT /NOMEM /LIST /REPORT	true	2.26	Win95/MS-D
NAVW.EXE	*.* /s	true	3.0	Win 3.1
WNAPVIR.EXE	/qm/m-/b- *.*	True	2.0	Win 3.1
WNCPAV.EXE	/qm/m-/b- *.*	True		Win 3.1
CPAV.EXE	*.* /p	true	1.1	MS-DOS
MSAV.EXE	*.* /p	true	Dist. WithMS-DOS 6.22	MS-DOS
WSCAN.EXE	%wscan	false	Prior to 9/97**	Win 3.1
IM.EXE	/N /UN /B /VL /RF=%f /P%d	false	3.21	MS-DOS

may come across compressed files in other formats, such as .ARJ, .ARC, .LZH, .TAR, .Z, .GZ, .TAZ, .TGZ and others.

ARJ and LHA are independent programs that can be installed to work with .ARJ and .LZH files (respectively) through WinZip's interface. Information on obtaining and installing these programs can be found in WinZip's Help file.

WinZip for Beginners

.ARC is an older compression format that is handled by several programs (listed in WinZip's Help file). WinZip itself, however, can perform almost any function upon .ARC files. The only thing WinZip can't do is add files to an .ARC archive. You need no external program to work with .ARC files.

You also do not require external programs to work with .TAR, .Z, .GZ, .TAZ or .TGZ files. Tape ARchive (.TAR) files are used only for organizing files; they are not compressed. The GZIP program creates .Z and .GZ compressed files. GZIP can only compress single files; it can not compress multiple files into a single archive. Both .TAZ and .TGZ files are created when .TAR files are compressed by GZIP. WinZip can perform most functions on each of these file types without the help of external programs. WinZip will not create archives in these formats, nor will it add files to an existing archive in these formats, but all of WinZip's other features can be used on them.

UUencode, XXencode, BinHex and MIME are used to transfer binary files via electronic mail. WinZip easily opens and extracts files in these formats. You may also convert an archive to UUencode format by selecting **Actions | UUencode** from WinZip's menu bar.

Using WinZip With Other Programs

If you have trouble sending e-mail attachments, try converting the file(s) into an UUencoded file and then sending.

Finally, the Microsoft Compress format (also known as LZEXPAND) is also recognized by WinZip. There are several variants of this format, so even though WinZip recognizes this format, you are limited to working with variants that are recognized by the version of Windows you are running (for example, Windows for Workgroups recognizes more variations of MSCompress than Windows 3.1). These archives only contain one file each, and usually end with an underscore, such as MSXXX.DL_ (though not all files ending with an underscore are LZEXPAND files).

Most people won't have occasion to need the other compression programs mentioned here. If you find you do need to work with .LZH or .ARJ files, the programs are easily obtained from the publishers or the internet. Remember, like WinZip, these programs are shareware.

WinZip's Internet Browser Support Add-on

The Internet Browser Support Add-on for WinZip automates downloading and opening ZIP files from the internet. Because Web browser technology changes so rapidly, this feature is not distributed as part of the WinZip package. You may download it from WinZip's Web site, at www.winzip.com/ibrowser.cgi. At 77K, this file downloads in less than 30 seconds with a 33.6kbps modem. After it is downloaded, run the self-extracting file, which will prompt you through installation. During installation you may specify the download folder into which WinZip will move the newly acquired files and decide whether WinZip will automatically open the archive.

Once installed, the IBSA works with Netscape and Microsoft browsers to automate downloads of ZIP files (the IBSA does not automatically act upon .EXE files). When a file finishes downloading, WinZip takes over and moves the file from the browser's temporary folder (which is emptied when you close the browser) to the folder you chose as the download folder. WinZip then opens the archive, where you may work with it like any other ZIP file.

After it is installed, the Internet Browser Support Add-on can operate totally hands free. You may double-click the Internet Browser Support Configuration icon in the WinZip directory to change settings for the add-on, or click **Options | Configure Internet Browser Support Add-on...** from WinZip's menu bar. Other than that, its operation is 100 percent automatic. Just sit back and let the downloads roll in.

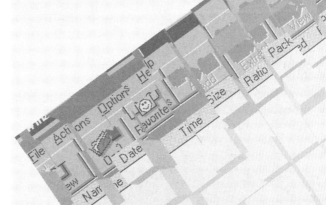

Chapter
14

WinZip
And The
Internet

WinZip for
Beginners

Since most ZIP files are transported on the internet, it's natural that WinZip is designed to make working with the internet easier. With or without the optional Internet Browser Support Add-on, WinZip works smoothly with your Web browser to ease downloads. WinZip is also an important tool for sending files attached to e-mail messages. Obviously, WinZip can be used to compress file attachments, so they take less time to transfer and occupy less bandwidth on the network. But WinZip can also be used to convert files into formats that can be sent under almost any internet conditions.

The WinZip Internet Browser Support Add-on (IBSA) can automate most of the steps involved in downloading, viewing and extracting compressed archives. Chapter 13 explains more details of this optional extra. Without this add-on, only a few simple steps are required to set your Web browser to automatically load WinZip when it is needed. Once these simple changes are made, your browser will load WinZip to decompress newly downloaded files.

WinZip And Netscape Navigator

After both programs have been installed, run Navigator and select **Options | General Preferences...** from the menu bar.

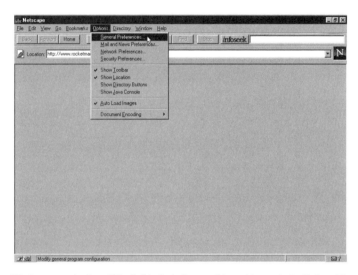

Click the Helpers tab. Highlight "application/zip" in the list box. If you do not see that entry, click [Create New Type...] and enter "application" as the MIME Type and "zip" or "winzip" as the Subtype.

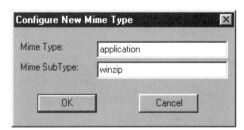

Enter all the file extensions WinZip will respond to in the File Extensions edit field (separate each by a comma—no spaces are necessary).

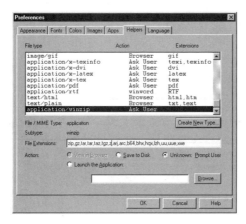

WinZip can handle all of the following types of files: ZIP, GZ, TAR, TAZ, TGZ, Z, ARJ, ARC, B64, BHX, HQX, LZH, UU, UUE, and XXE. Next, click the "Launch the Application" radio button and browse to your WinZip program file (C:\PROGRAM FILES\WINZIP\WINZIP32.EXE, if you followed the default installation in Windows 95). Next time you download a file having one of these extensions, Netscape will launch WinZip when the download is complete, and WinZip will open the archive for you.

WinZip And Microsoft Internet Explorer

People using Internet Explorer may find that WinZip is already set to respond to compressed files. This happens because Windows and Internet Explorer share the same program associations. If WinZip and Internet Explorer are not already linked, it is very simple to do so. After both are installed, launch Internet Explorer and click **View | Options...** from the menu bar.

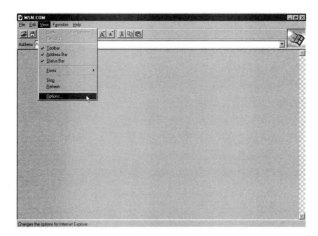

Select the File Types tab. Browse the list for WinZip.

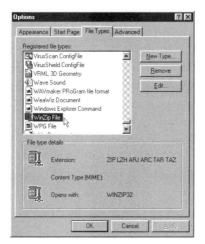

If it's there, click on it to see what files are associated to bring up WinZip. If it's not there, click [New Type...]. Enter a description of the file type (such as "WinZip files") and the associated file extensions: ZIP, GZ, TAR, TAZ, TGZ, Z, ARJ, ARC, B64, BHX, HQX, LZH, UU, UUE, and XXE. At the bottom of the page, click [New] to define the action and enter "OPEN." Click [OK] when you are done.

Now Internet Explorer will open WinZip when you download a file that has any of the associated file extensions.

Using WinZip With E-mail

Sending and receiving electronic mail (e-mail) is the most popular use of the internet. It is, has, and will be so for a long time. E-mail can reach anywhere in the world almost instantly for just pennies. Because of its convenience and affordability, it is quickly replacing the telephone as the preferred means of communication for many people, just as the telephone has largely eclipsed letter writing.

E-mail also lets users send computer files across the internet. Usually these are sent as attachments to e-mail messages. Write to friends about a recent vacation to the islands and attach photos of shimmering waters and sandy beaches to that e-mail.

An obvious use of WinZip is to compress those photos into an archive before attaching them. This lets you attach one file instead of many, and reduces the transit time between you and your friends.

But some e-mail programs have trouble transferring files across the internet. Some proprietary on-line services will only let users send files to other members of that service.

One reason for these problems is that the internet can only carry ASCII text characters (like those on your keyboard). It can not carry binary files, which include most program and data files. All files attached to e-mail messages are converted into text, shipped across the 'net, then decoded back to their original state. At least that's what happens when everything works properly. But maybe you've received a message that contained a block of garbled text.

```
_=_
_=_ Part 001 of 001 of file encoded.txt
_=_
begin 666 encoded.txt
M5&5S="="$-"@T*1V5N=&QE(%)E861E<CH-"@T*5&AI<R!I<R!N;W1H:6YG(&UO
M<F4@=&AA;B!A('1E<W0@9FEL92!C<F5A=&5D('1O('!R;W9I9&4@9F]D9&5R
M(&9O<B!T:&4@=&%R%R:6]U<R!E;F-O9&EN9R!S8VAE;65S+B!)9B!Y;W4@87)E
M('5S:6YG(&ET('1O('1E<W0@=&QL(&-O;F=R871U;&%T:6]N;!Y;W5R(&%G;&
M:6QI=D@:6X@:6X8W55T=&EN9R!RP@<&%S=&EN9R!RP<V%V:6YG+"!A;F0@9&5C;V1I
M:;F<@=&-I<F@=7-VEN6FEP+%T'*#0!0I%;%;FIO>2$`
end
```

This is an example of an attachment that wasn't properly decoded into its binary format. UUencoding is one method of converting binary files into text, which a recipient can decode into its original form.

If you've been having trouble sending or receiving attachments, WinZip may be able to help you. You can sidestep some problems by UUencoding an archive before sending it. This is easily done with WinZip.

Open or create an archive in WinZip. When you are ready, select **Actions | UUencode** in the menu bar.

This creates a .UUE file in the same directory as the ZIP with which you are working. This .UUE file can be sent as an attachment with most e-mail programs (usually with a Send File or Attach File command). If you still have trouble, try opening the .UUE file in a text editor (such as Windows Notepad). Select all of the text and copy it to the Windows Clipboard (Ctrl + C). Then return to the open e-mail you are about to send and paste the material directly into the e-mail (Ctrl + V). If the recipient of this message is an internet novice, you may also want to include instructions on decoding the UUE information.

WinZip for Beginners

Receiving attachments is also easy with WinZip. WinZip can open and extract UUencode, XXencode, BinHex and MIME formats, though it sometimes needs a little help. If you receive an attachment in an e-mail message, re-save the file as a UUE file. In many e-mail programs this is done by selecting **File | Save as...** from the menu bar, then changing the file extension (the three letters after the period) to UUE. Another option is to copy the coded information to a text editor and then save it as UUE.

Some other e-mail programs will save the attachment as a file separate from the e-mail itself. In these cases, you may need to rename the file with the UUE ending (this may be done with a Save As... operation or by right-clicking the file and selecting **Rename** from the context menu). If the file was split into multiple files (some programs prefer to send several small messages instead of one large e-mail), use a text editor to cut and paste them into a single file. Once you have a single UUE file, open it in WinZip like any other archive. If the file is already in one of the recognized file formats when it arrives, WinZip should be ready to detect the method used and decode it for you.

The most common problems encountered with attached files are incomplete data and missing header information, both of which can have several causes. If you have trouble, helpful examples of each protocol can be found in WinZip's Help under the Hints, Tips and Troubleshooting topic. See your e-mail program's documentation for more information on attaching files.

Chapter 15

WinZip Options

WinZip is powerful and popular because its extensive options allow you to customize WinZip. Most programs have user-configurable options, but these usually require the user to dig deeply into the program, and sometimes even to use arcane command line parameters: typing code characters at the end of the run command. But WinZip makes this easy for you, even providing you with an **Options** menu command.

This is a powerful list of choices. Spending just a few minutes looking over your options can make WinZip even easier to use and optimize the program for the way you use it. Place a checkmark (by clicking) before the options you wish to activate.

Configuration...

The Configuration dialog box controls WinZip's default actions, appearance and more.

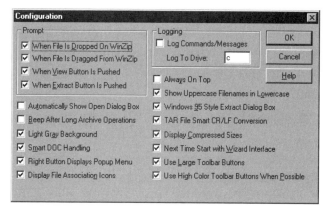

Beginning in the upper left, you decide when WinZip will prompt you for permission before acting. When disabled, WinZip will perform the action without displaying a dialog box.

* **When File Is Dropped On WinZip**: This option applies to adding files to an archive by dragging and dropping them onto WinZip's program window. When disabled (no checkmark), WinZip adds the file using the options last specified in the Drop dialog box.

* **When File Dragged From WinZip**: When disabled, the file being dragged will be extracted using the options from the most recent Extract dialog box.

* **When View Button Is Pushed**: This determines whether or not you will be prompted with the View dialog box when the View toolbar button is clicked. This option does not apply to the **Actions | View** menu command.

* **When Extract Button Is Pushed**: If this is disabled, the options from the previous Extract dialog box will be put into effect when the Extract toolbar button is clicked. This option does not apply to the **Actions | Extract** menu command.

Each of these prompt options can be toggled with the (Shift) key. For example, if WinZip is set to display a dialog box when you drag and drop a file onto the WinZip window, pressing (Shift) as you drop the file will bypass the dialog prompt.

You also have the option of recording WinZip's messages and commands to a log file. When activated, WinZip will maintain a log of all errors WinZip encounters and all commands WinZip issues to external programs. You may specify the drive to which this log is written. You'll find it as WINZIP.LOG in the root of the selected drive (for instance, if C: is the selected drive, the report will be at C:\WINZIP.LOG).

The Configuration dialog box also determines many other aspects of WinZip:

* **Automatically Show Open Dialog Box**: When active, this option automatically displays the Open dialog box when WinZip is started.

* **Beep After Long Archive Operations**: When selected, WinZip will beep after completing archive operations that last more than one second.

* **Light Gray Background**: Use this option to select light or dark gray for the program window background.

* **Smart DOC Handling**: This allows WinZip to launch one of two programs to view files having the DOC extension. If the file is simple ASCII text characters, WinZip will open the Default Association program (specified in the Program Locations dialog box) to view the file. If the file contains word processor information (like italics or headers), WinZip will open the associated program. When active, this option avoids the overhead of loading a large word processing program only to view a simple text document.

* **Right Button Displays Popup Menu**: This determines whether clicking the right mouse button on a file in the archive window opens a context menu or is used to select the file (just as the left button would).

* **Display File Association Icons**: This will display an icon beside each file in the archive window to indicate executable files or associated programs.

* **Always On Top**: This prevents the WinZip program window from being overlaid by other program windows on the desktop.

* **Show Uppercase Filenames in Lowercase**: This may improve the readability of file names in the archive window by changing all-caps file names into lower-case characters.

* **Windows 95 Style Extract Dialog Box**: On 32-bit systems, this determines whether the Extract dialog box will contain a tree-view control or use the Windows 3.1-style folder control.

* **TAR File Smart CR/LF Conversion**: "CR/LF" represents "Carriage Return/Line Feed." Some computer systems, like Macintosh and Unix, use a carriage return or a line feed (respectively) to end a line in a text file. Windows programs, however, usually require both a carriage return and a line feed. This option looks at the first 80 characters in a TAR file to determine if it is a text file. If so, it converts single carriage returns and line feeds into CR/LF pairs, so that the file may be read accurately by a Windows text editor.

* **Display Compressed Sizes**: If you wish to display the files' compressed sizes and compression ratios in the archive window, check this option.

* **Next Time Start with Wizard Interface**: The Wizard interface will be active next time WinZip is run when this box is checked.

* **Use Large Toolbar Buttons**: Use this option to select large or slightly smaller buttons in the WinZip toolbar.

* **Use High Color Toolbar Buttons When Possible**: When active, WinZip will display high-color toolbar buttons on capable systems. (This is only available when using large buttons.)

Folders...

In the Folders dialog box you may choose the directories that WinZip works with during zipping and unzipping operations.

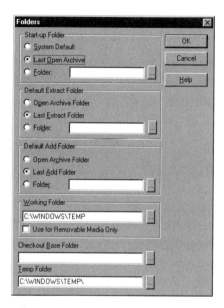

The first option is for the Start-up Folder. This is the default directory WinZip displays in the dialog box when opening or creating an archive.

* The **System Default** uses the folder containing the WinZip program file.

* When the **Last Open Archive** is selected, WinZip will use the folder containing the last archive that was opened (unless that was from the A: or B: drive).

* You may choose another directory by selecting the **Folder:** option and specifying the folder. Use the [...] button to browse the hard drive.

The Default Extract Folder is the next item in the Folders dialog box. This specifies the folder that WinZip automatically opens when you extract a file.

* Selecting the **Open Archive Folder** will extract the archive into the folder containing the ZIP file.

* **Last Extract Folder** uses the same directory that received the latest extraction.

* You may select another directory by choosing the **Folder:** option. Click the [...] button to browse the hard drive.

You may choose which folder is opened for Add operations in the Default Add Folder area.

* When **Open Archive Folder** is selected, the folder containing the open ZIP file is used by default for Add operations.

* Select **Last Add Folder** to use the same directory that was chosen in the last Add dialog box.

* Select **Folder:** to specify another directory. Click the [...] button to browse.

WinZip uses the Working Folder to hold temporary files used when carrying out your commands. If no directory is specified, WinZip will use the folder containing the open archive. A working folder is useful when updating archives on drives that don't have enough room for both the original and the updated archives (for example, on a floppy disk). In fact, you may opt to use the specified folder only when working on removable media (like floppy disks). To enable this, simply check the box next to "Use For Removable Media Only."

WinZip uses the Checkout Base Folder as the default prefix in the CheckOut dialog box. When you run a CheckOut operation, WinZip needs a folder to extract the files to temporarily. The folder selected here will be the base path for those temporary files. If no directory is chosen, WinZip will use the folder containing the open archive.

The Temp Folder, usually the same one used by Windows, is used for temporary files, such as those created during a virus scan. If you receive an error citing low disk space during one of these operations, try changing the Temp directory to a drive with more free space.

Explorer Configuration...

Here you set how WinZip interacts with Windows Explorer.

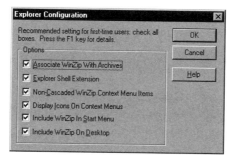

* Enabling **Associate WinZip With Archives** allows you to open the following archives in WinZip by double-clicking them in Explorer: ZIP, LZH, ARJ, ARC, TAR, TGZ, TAZ, GZ, Z, UU, UUE, XXE, B64, HQX, BHX.

* Selecting **Explorer Shell Extension** will enable the WinZip context (right-click) menus in Explorer and allow you to use drag-and-drop to zip and unzip files without leaving Explorer.

* **Non-Cascaded WinZip Context Menu Items** determines whether the WinZip context menu entries are all listed in the main context menu or are listed in a WinZip sub-menu.

* When **Display Icons On Context Menus** is selected, the WinZip entries in Explorer's context menus will appear with WinZip icons.

* Selecting **Include WinZip In Start Menu** will place a shortcut to WinZip in the Windows 95 Start menu.

* When active, the **Include WinZip On Desktop** option will place a WinZip shortcut icon on the desktop.

File Manager Configuration...

If you are running WinZip with Windows 3.x or NT, you may configure it to your File Manager.

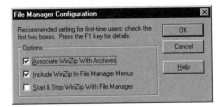

* Enable **Associate WinZip With Archives** to use WinZip for actions upon ZIP, LZH, ARJ, ARC, TAR, TGZ, TAZ, GZ, Z, UU, UUE, XXE, B64, HQX and BHX files.

* Select **Include WinZip in File Manager Menus** to insert a WinZip menu in File Manager's menu bar.

* If you wish to load and close WinZip each time you start and stop the File Manager, enable the **Start & Stop WinZip With File Manager** option.

Configure Internet Browser Support Add-on...

If you have installed the optional (and free) Internet Browser Support Add-on, you can set its options in this dialog box. In the Configuration area, click the first option to automatically move downloaded files to the specified folder. Click the second option to automatically open newly downloaded ZIP files in WinZip. If you wish to change the folder to which files are automatically moved after downloading, click the [Change Download Folder...] button.

Lower down, you can click the (Check Compatibility Info On Web Site) button to launch your browser software and visit WinZip's Web site to check the latest details on compatibility between WinZip's IBSA and Web browsers.

Font...

You may also select the font that WinZip displays in the archive window. Select your preferred font on the left, the style in the middle and the size on the right. You may preview your choice in the Sample window. If available, you may also choose a different script at the bottom of the window. This can be a fun option to experiment with, but most users will find the default font to be the easiest to read.

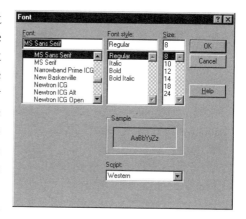

Program Locations...

This is explained in detail in chapter 13.

Sort

This option lets you arrange the files in WinZip's archive window by one of eight criteria. The files may be listed by name (alphabetically), Path, file Type, Size (before compression), Packed Size (after zipping), Compression Ratio, Date or the Original Order in which they were zipped.

Clicking on the archive window header is another way to sort by the items listed.

Reuse WinZip Windows

This toggle option determines whether WinZip will use one window or if it will open a new window every time you open another archive by double-clicking in Explorer.

Save Settings on Exit
Save Settings Now

These allow you to save information which will be restored next time you start WinZip. The first will save the active settings when you exit WinZip, restoring them when you start it again. The second will immediately save the current settings, restoring them when you start it again.

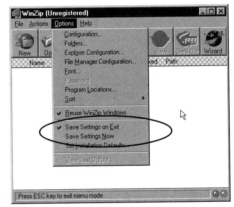

This applies to all the settings in the Options menu, all those in Add, Configure and Extract dialog boxes, and the size and location of WinZip's program window. (The options in the Folders and Program Locations dialogs are saved regardless.)

Set Installation Defaults...

This option allows you to restore the program options and folder names to the original installation defaults.

View Last Output...

This will display the results of the last command issued by WinZip, for example, to a virus scanner or other external program.

Appendix A

Menu Commands

Most actions in WinZip can be achieved in several ways. The menu bar is just one of these. Most of these same actions can also be accomplished with right-clicks, drag-and-drop, toolbar buttons or keyboard shortcuts.

The results of each of these menu commands are explained in more detail in the relevant chapter of this book. This list is provided as a reference.

Menu commands that end with an ellipse '...' open a dialogue or prompt box before executing an action. Those without ellipses perform the associated action immediately.

File

* **New Archive...**: Create a new zipped file with WinZip. ([Ctrl] + [N])

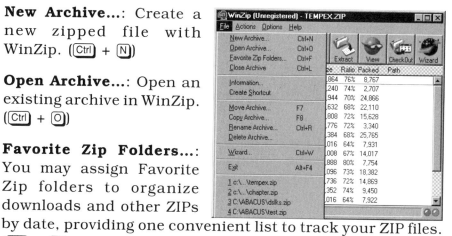

* **Open Archive...**: Open an existing archive in WinZip. ([Ctrl] + [O])

* **Favorite Zip Folders...**: You may assign Favorite Zip folders to organize downloads and other ZIPs by date, providing one convenient list to track your ZIP files. ([Ctrl] + [F])

* **Close Archive**: Closes the open archive. Both **New Archive...** and **Open Archive...** automatically close the open archive before opening the next. ([Ctrl] + [L])

* **Information...**: This displays a dialogue box listing the archive format, full filename, size of the ZIP, number of files it contains, the average compression ratio of those files, and the date and time the archive was last updated.

* **Create Shortcut**: Creates a shortcut on the desktop to the open archive.

* **Move Archive...**: This will move an archive from its current location into another, which you specify in the dialogue box. ([F7])

* **Copy Archive...**: This creates a copy of the open archive. Select its location in the dialog box. ([F8])

* **Rename Archive...**: This allows you to rename the open archive. After selecting this command, type the new name and click [OK]. ([Ctrl] + [R])

* **Delete Archive...**: Move the open archive into Windows's Recycle Bin.

* **Wizard...**: This switches WinZip to the Wizard interface. ([Ctrl] + [W])

* **Mail Archive**: Available only in configurations that include MAPI.DLL, this makes it easy to electronically mail ZIP archives to other people. ([Ctrl] + [M])

* **Exit**: This closes the WinZip program window. ([Alt] + [F 4])

* **1, 2, 3...**: You may re-open recently opened archives from the File menu. The archives' names will be listed next to the numbers.

Actions

* **Add...**: Add files to the open archive. ([Ctrl] + [A])

* **Delete...**: Delete files from the open archive. ([Ctrl] + [D])

* **Extract...**: Unzips the open archive to a directory of your choice. ([Ctrl] + [E])

* **View...**: View a file in the open archive. ([Ctrl] + [V])

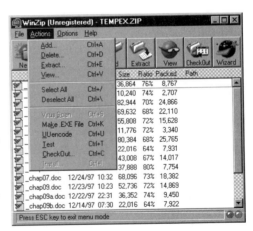

* **Select All**: Select every file in the open archive to perform an action upon. (Ctrl + /)

* **Deselect All**: Unselect all the files in the open archive. (Ctrl + \\)

* **Virus Scan**: Run an external anti-virus program upon the contents of the open archive. (Ctrl + S)

* **Make .EXE File**: Create a copy of the open archive as a self-extracting executable file. (Ctrl + K)

* **UUencode**: Convert a file into the UUencoded format. (Ctrl + U)

* **Test**: Test the open ZIP file to ensure it contains no errors. (Ctrl + T)

* **CheckOut...**: Examine or run files in the open archive. (Ctrl + C)

* **Install...**: Run the archive's INSTALL or SETUP program. (Ctrl + I)

Options

* **Configuration...**: Summons the dialogue box to set WinZip's configuration options.

* **Folders...**: Specify the default folders WinZip uses when working with archives.

* **Explorer Configuration...**: Under Windows 95/NT, this summons the dialogue box where you set how WinZip and the Windows Explorer cooperate.

WinZip for Beginners

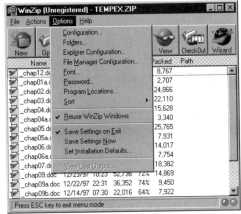

* **File Manager Configuration...**: Specify how WinZip works with the File Manager.

* **Configure Internet Browser Support Add-on...**: With the optional IBSA installed, you may use this dialogue box to determine its behavior.

* **Font...**: Choose the font, style and size of the letters used in WinZip's archive window.

* **Password...**: You may set passwords to secure the information in zipped archives.

* **Program Locations...**: Specify the programs (and their locations) with which WinZip will work, such as virus scanners and file viewers.

* **Sort**: You may sort the files listed in WinZip's archive window by name, path, file type, size, packed size, compression ratio, date or the original order in which they were zipped.

* **Reuse WinZip Windows**: This determines whether you use the same WinZip window when opening or creating another archive, or if a new WinZip window is opened for each operation.

* **Save Settings on Exit**: Enable this option to save the current options and location of the WinZip window when WinZip is closed. These will be used next time you start WinZip.

* **Save Settings Now**: Immediately save the current options to be used next time WinZip is loaded.

* **Set Installation Defaults...**: Restores original installation defaults for many options.

* **View Last Output...**: View the output from the last command issued by WinZip.

Help

* **Contents**: Open the WinZip Help file and display the topics covered.

* **Brief Tutorial**: Take a few minutes to learn the basics of using WinZip with this ten-step tutorial.

* **Hints and Tips**: Display hints and tips to get the most out of WinZip.

* **Search for Help on...**: Open the search dialogue to find what you need in WinZip's Help file.

* **How to Use Help**: View the Contents tab to display instructions for using the Help system.

* **Frequently Asked Questions**: View answers to commonly asked questions about WinZip, either in the Help file or at WinZip's Web site.

WinZip for Beginners

* **Ordering Information**: View details on registering your copy of WinZip, either in the Help file or at WinZip's Web site.

* **WinZip Home Page**: If you have an internet connection, you may visit WinZip's Web page.

* **About WinZip...**: Display the copyright information and version number of your copy of WinZip.

Appendix B

Command Line Parameters

Some advanced users may wish to take advantage of WinZip's command line parameters. These allow users to enter additional information at the Run command. WinZip uses this information to perform specific actions upon files without needing any additional prompting in the program window. Most users won't want to bother with these commands, but they are included here for those who find them useful.

Adding Files

To add files to an archive from the command line, use the following format precisely:

```
WINZIP[32].EXE  ACTION  [OPTIONS]  FILENAME[.ZIP]  FILES
```

Elements in brackets '[]' are optional (but if you are running the 32-bit version of WinZip, be sure the "32" is in WinZip's filename).

Action

The action tells WinZip what you want it to do. These actions correspond to those in the Add dialog box.

* **-A**: Add files to the archive.

* **-F**: Freshen files in the archive.

* **-U**: Update files in the archive.

* **-M**: Move files into the archive.

These commands are explained more fully in chapter eight and in WinZip's Help file.

Options

The available options correspond to those found in the Add dialog box. All of these are optional. You may use as many as are relevant (separate each by a space).

* **-R**: Activates the Recurse Directories option.

* **-P**: Activates the Save Extra Directory Information option.

* **-EX**: Uses maximum compression.

* **-EN**: Uses normal compression (default).

* **-EF**: Uses fast compression.

* **-ES**: Uses superfast compression.

* **-E0**: Doesn't compress the files.

* **-HS**: Includes hidden and system files.

* **-SPassword**: Specify a case-sensitive password to protect the archive (replace "Password" with your preferred password). The password may be placed in quotes, such as: -S"Secret Password."

Filename.zip

Specify the ZIP file you are working with. Be sure to include the full path and filename, for example:

```
C:\DOWNLOADS\FILENAME.ZIP.
```

Files

This is a list of files you wish to add to FILENAME.ZIP, or enter the "@" character followed by the filename containing a list of files to add. The latter is useful when moving files among archives. Wildcards (such as "*") are acceptable here.

Example

Click **Start | Run...** and enter:

```
WINZIP32.EXE    -A    -HS    -S"NO ACCESS"    C:\TEST1.ZIP
C:\TEMP\*.TXT
```

In this Windows 95 example, I'm adding all the text files (*.TXT) in the C:\TEMP directory to the TEST1 archive in the root directory of the "C" drive. I've instructed WinZip to include any system or hidden files (-HS) and to guard the archive with the password "No Access."

Extracting Files

The format for extracting ZIPs from the command line is:

```
WINZIP[32].EXE  -E  [OPTIONS]  FILENAME[.ZIP]  DIRECTORY
```

-E

This is required; it tells WinZip that you wish to extract an archive according to the following specifications. Details on extracting files are explained in chapter seven.

Options

These are similar to the options you specify in the Extract dialog box.

* **-O**: This represents "Overwrite existing files without prompting."

* **-J**: This equates to "Junk pathnames." If this isn't used, WinZip extracts with the directory information stored in the archive.

* **-SPassword**: Use this option to specify a case-sensitive password. As before, this may also be enclosed in quotation marks.

Filename.zip

This specifies the file you wish to extract. Remember to include the full directory path to the file.

Directory

This is the directory into which the archived files will be extracted. This directory will be created if it doesn't already exist.

Example

To extract files from the command line, click **Start | Run...** and type:

```
WINZIP32.EXE  -E  -O  C:\TEST1.ZIP  C:\TEMP
```

This runs WinZip, which automatically extracts the contents of the TEST1 compressed archive into the C:\TEMP directory. I've enabled the "-O" option to overwrite any preexisting files that have the same name as the files being extracted.

Important Notes

* Always specify complete filenames, including the full directory path and drive letter.

* You may run WinZip minimized by using the "-MIN" option. When used, this must be the first option listed.

* Separate the action and each option by at least one space character.

* Enclose long filenames (longer than eight characters, plus three for the file extension) in quotation marks.

* Only operations involving WinZip's built-in zip and unzip features are supported by command line parameters.

Appendix C

WinZip for Beginners Glossary

Add:

The process of placing files into a ZIP file.

Archive:

(1) A file containing one or more compressed files. (2) To compress files into an archive.

Archive Window:

The area of WinZip's program window which displays files in an archive.

ASCII:

American Standard Code for Information Interchange, a system of digital keyboard characters.

Associate:

To tell your computer what programs should be used to open what types of files.

WinZip for Beginners Glossary

Beta:

A pre-release version of software. This is usually the final testing version before the official release of a program.

Browser:

A program used to access and view information from the World Wide Web (also known as a "Web Browser").

Classic:

One of two interfaces WinZip offers. The Classic interface provides the most features and power to the user.

Command Line:

The text that is entered in the Run dialogue box or at the DOS prompt to run a program.

Compress:

To reduce the size of files by removing unnecessary data, which is restored when the file is decompressed. This is the same as zipping.

Compression Ratio:

This shows how much smaller the compressed file is than the original.

Context Menu:

The pop-up menu that appears when one right-clicks the mouse in Windows Explorer.

Decompress:

To restore a compressed file to its original state. This is the same as unzipping.

Dialogue Box:

A window that lets you enter information a program will use to perform the action you command, or to confirm your request.

WinZip for Beginners

Directory:

Files are stored in directories (sometimes within other directories) on your computer. These may also be called "folders."

Download:

(1) To copy a file from the internet onto your computer. (2) A file that has been copied from the internet.

Drag and Drop:

(1) A computer interface which allows you to click on an item with the mouse, "drag" it elsewhere on the computer screen and drop it into a new location. (2) To click on a file with the mouse, "drag" it to another location and release it there.

Extract:

To decompress, or unzip, the files in an archive.

File Extension:

The three letters after the period in a computer file's name. This usually indicates what type of file it is.

Freshen:

Found in WinZip's Add dialogue box, this command will update the files within an archive.

Internet Browser Support Add-on:

An optional program that plugs into WinZip to automate the way WinZip handles downloads with your Web browser.

Nico Mak Computing, Inc.:

Creator and publisher of WinZip.

Pack:

To zip files into an archive.

WinZip for Beginners Glossary

Register:

To pay for the use of WinZip, making you a legal user of the program, upon which you will receive the latest version of WinZip, a print manual and technical support when needed.

Self-extracting Archive:

Self-extracting archives are zipped files that can be run as programs. When one is run, it extracts itself, with no need for an unzipping program.

Shareware:

Programs that are distributed free of charge. The user may evaluate the program for a limited time, usually thirty days. After this time, the user is required to register with the program's publisher or discontinue using the program. Shareware allows users to try software before buying, and keeps prices low by avoiding the retail channel.

Spanning:

Many occasions require one to create zipped files onto removable storage media, like floppy disks. But often, a single floppy isn't large enough to hold the entire ZIP file. Spanning allows one to create a ZIP file that spans across several floppy disks.

Unpack:

To decompress, or unzip, an archive.

Unzip:

To extract, or decompress, an archive.

UUencode:

A protocol for converting binary files (like computer programs) into text. This allows files of any sort to be transported across the internet. The receiver then uses a UUencode program to convert the text back into binary characters.

WinZip for Beginners

Virus Scanner:

A program that scans computer files looking for evidence of computer viruses.

Wildcard:

Some computer programs let you use wildcard characters ('*' or '?') to replace text that may change or take several variants. For instance, "beck*" could represent both "becky" and "becki."

WinZip:

The most popular data compression program available, published by Nico Mak Computing, Inc.

Wizard:

One of two interfaces WinZip offers. The Wizard helps you unzip files with a few clearly explained mouse clicks.

Zip:

To compress files into an archive.

ZIP:

The typical file extension of a compressed file; may also refer to a compressed archive.

Index

Z

PC catalog

Order Toll Free 1-800-451-4319
Books and Software

PC INTERN
SYSTEM PROGRAMMING 6th Edition

PC memory organization
Extended & expanded memory
COM & EXE programs
DOS structures and functions
BIOS interrupts
Programming video cards
TSR programs

Abacus
A Data Becker Book

Michael Tischer

DATA BECKER EDITION

Tischer 282

INCLUDES COMPACT DISK WITH SAMPLE PROGRAMS

Abacus

www.abacuspub.com

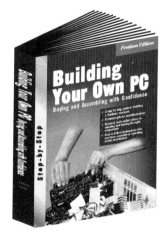

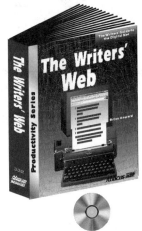

Don't Forget To Visit Our Website

Now you can find all the latest information about Abacus and Abacus products at our website: **http://www.abacuspub.com**.

The Abacus website includes an online catalog so you can find out what you need to know about a title. You can also preview upcoming books and software. Have a question you need answered? Send E-mail to our technical staff, customer service reps and editors right from our web site.

The website shows how you can order Abacus products; you can even order online over the Internet directly from Abacus.

If you have a question or a problem with one of our books or software titles, we may already have the answer for you. Our FAQs are arranged under "Books" and "Software" icons. Simply click the desired icon to see the information.

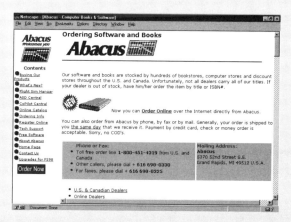

Thank you for buying WinZip for Beginners. We hope this book will be an indispensable reference guide to using WinZip 6.3. You have two methods of installing WinZip from the companion CD-ROM.

Method 1

* Insert the WinZip for Beginners companion CD-ROM in the CD-ROM drive of your computer.

* Click [Start] and select the **Run...** command to open the Run dialog box.

* Type D:\SETUP.EXE in the dialog box and click [OK]. (Substitute your CD-ROM drive letter if it is different.)

This begins the WinZip installation wizard. See Chapter 2 for information on completing the WinZip installation.

Method 2

Another method to install WinZip is to use the companion CD-ROM menu procedure. This is especially important for Windows 3.x users. Insert the companion CD-ROM in the CD-ROM drive of your PC.

* Insert the WinZip for Beginners companion CD-ROM in the CD-ROM drive of your computer.

* Click [Start] and select the **Run...** command to open the Run dialog box.

* Type D:\SETUP.EXE in the dialog box and click [OK]. (Substitute your CD-ROM drive letter if it is different.)

Windows 95 users

Click the "Click Here to install WinZip Win 95 Evaluation Copy" icon. Then following the on-screen prompts.

Windows 3.x users

Click the "Click Here to install WinZip Win 3.x Evaluation Copy" icon. Then following the on-screen prompts.